VISTA B

THE VIEW FROM HERE

David Challice was born in 1960 in Brighton,
England. He has had a varied career...running
"Strip & Wax" his own furniture restoration
business, freelance journalism, and more
recently administering the head office of the
UK Independence Party.
He lives with his partner in a cottage on the
edge of Dartmoor. The View From Here is his
first book.

THE VIEW FROM HERE

DAVID CHALLICE

ISBN 978-0-9558091-0-1

VISTA BOOKS

THE VIEW FROM HERE

VISTA BOOKS

Published by VISTA BOOKS
Head Office
Astarte House
1 Vale Drive
Midanbury
Southampton
SO18 4SW
vistapublishing@btinternet.com

FIRST EDITION MARCH 2008

Typesetting and Cover Design by **ASTARTE DIGITAL** www.astartedigital.com

Set in Bookman Old Style.

Print Management provided by Print by Design Ltd, Bodmin, Cornwall.
www.printbydesign.co.uk

INTRODUCTION

The Trago Mills column has become something of an institution in the South-West of England. Originally written by Mike Robertson, founder of the successful Trago stores, it first emerged as Tripehound, sniffing out tripe wherever it lay. Sometimes controversial, always unique, Mike's aims were to alert his readers to things going on behind their backs and motivating them into doing something about it.

Over the years Mike wrote hundreds of Tripehound pieces, which appeared in newspapers large and small, with a dedicated readership. But in 2001, as his health declined, he stepped down, in the hope that others would come forward to take up the reins. It was at that point in May 2001 – incensed at the conduct of the Labour Government's handling of Foot & Mouth disease - that I volunteered my first contribution. I never expected to be here six years later.

They say that the best way of learning is to teach. I can vouch for that. Researching these articles has led me to open a number of boxes I would never normally have approached. Sometimes I quickly closed the lid, restricting myself to the main theme of "Britain can survive outside the EU perfectly happily." That task is huge enough without overloading the mules. But it's not all about the EU, as you will see.

The pieces are in date order. I have made a few minor changes, particularly when – with hindsight – I felt I had started to waffle. These were early pieces from 2001 and have simply been slimmed down a little.

This is a retrospective so I have not amended any individual's names or the official positions they held at the time, which would get tedious and look forced. Gordon Brown, for example, is usually referred to as Chancellor Brown, rather than former Chancellor.

I have avoided selective editing just to make myself look better. Where I have made predictions, these are included in the text. Sometimes they turned out to be wrong ("Tony Blair won't give us a referendum on the Constitution; he will bring it in by the back door"... It was Gordon Brown who did that). But the predictions have usually proved to be accurate. I write this in sadness more than triumph.

I should also explain why Exeter and Ben Bradshaw feature so prominently. When I wrote the book I lived in that city and Mr Bradshaw was my MP.

It would be wrong not mention that a handful of other writers (including Godfrey Bloom MEP) have contributed to the Trago Column over the years, and I'm grateful to them. Bruce Robertson, owner of Trago Mills, also pays thanks to them in his tribute (below) to his father, Mike, who passed away in November 2001.

DEDICATED TO MIKE ROBERTSON

who started it all

CONTENTS

2004

2005

2007 *(continued)*

2001

AS THE CARCASSES BURN

British livestock farming could be facing total collapse. The first casualties of Foot and Mouth have been in Cumbria, Galloway and Devon but it is likely that the rest of the country may be dragged down the same terrible route.

Virulent as a medieval plague, the impact of the disease has spread beyond the farmyard to county councils, leisure, tourism, hauliers and rural shopkeepers. Even car boot sales and Crufts have been cancelled. Whatever spin the Prime Minister imparts, the countryside is not open for business. In anyone's language, this is a crisis, and not 'under control'.

The ultimate measure of any Government is, does it cope in an emergency? Can it mobilise and deal with a threat? New Labour is a party of the city. They understand how cities work, hence their landslide victory in '97. But every coin has two sides. New Labour's fear and ignorance of the countryside is deeply damaging to the national interest.

To their credit, many Labour MP's regard their own party's response as 'clueless'. Stories of MAFF officials telephoning timber suppliers, enquiring on the availability of pallets in case of an outbreak of Foot and Mouth – two weeks before the disease struck – must undermine the Government's credibility. Did they know that Foot and Mouth was on its way?

This is bad enough. More worrying is that the European Union wants British farming to go belly up, offering grants to UK farmers to leave agriculture. Presumably these families will then be employed as pastoral furniture, populating the landscape as exhibits in a living museum?

With EU expansion to the East, Poland is now designated the agricultural area of Europe. Conspiracy theory? Perhaps. But consider the destruction of the UK fishing industry with our boats smashed up on the shoreline. And now it's probably the turn of British farming. Between a smiling Prime Minister, and Nick Brown - the Minister who appears to be a 'speak your weight' machine, unblinking and monotone (though he probably blinked in '97 when told that he was to be 'given' Agriculture) - we can only watch the fiddling as the carcasses burn.

May 2001

TONY BLAIR IN A STOVEPIPE HAT

Tony Blair makes no secret of the fact that he is determined to scrap the Pound Sterling in favour of the euro. We don't need the old currency. Like yards and miles, the pound is ancient, an anachronism, as relevant to modern Europe as penny-farthing bicycles or policemen in stovepipe hats. The past is history, the future is orange.

Well perhaps. But the Prime Minister has one major problem. While he's preparing to parachute into the heart of Europe, 70% of us disagree with him. The euro is a bridge too far.

Mr Blair must find this intensely frustrating. How can he hold a referendum on the single currency when he knows that the People will come back to him with the 'wrong' answer? He cannot, of course. Losing would be unthinkable. A political depth-charge. In all likelihood he will delay the referendum until after the next General Election, in 2007 or thereabouts.

At the heart of this there lies a fundamental difference of opinion over the very idea of the nation state, over what it is to be a 'country'. Civil wars have been fought over less. And when a government feels embarrassed at the history of its own country, apologising for everything from the slave trade to the Empire, it becomes disturbing.

As for Britain joining the euro, it's not like joining the Caravan Club. We cannot simply walk away if we don't like it. Loss of currency means loss of political control. Our gold reserves will be controlled by Frankfurt and we will lose control of interest rates, taxation and government spending.

Would the Americans give up their dollar? The Japanese their yen? If we sign up for the euro, the final ingredients for disaster will have been assembled. We will have shackled ourselves, losing our freedom to trade with the world and to choose our own path. As a nation we will be history; finished. We must be blind... or mad.

June 2001

APATHY PARTY FAILS TO STAND IN ELECTION

In the poem 'Polling Day' Vernon Scannell confessed to mixed feelings in the voting booth when making his selection on the ballot paper. He ended with the perfect line: 'So oddly apt this cross, illiterate kiss'. But still he voted.

Thirty years later, things are different. In the 2001 general election it has become clear that the landslide winner was the Apathy Party.

At least 40% of our fellow-voters have sunk into a state of torpor. While the rest of us engaged in the privilege of a general election, the Apathy Party stayed at home, lumped in front of the telly, indifferent and passionless, more interested in Wheel of Fortune or the Weakest Link than in who runs the country.

During the actual counting of votes on 7th June, Ben Bradshaw MP saw nothing wrong, shrugging away the lowest turnout since 1918 as 'an apathy of contentment'. Everybody knew he was going to win. Unless people really disliked him why should they even bother to vote?

It's probably best to pass over this without comment, but the other explanations are no more convincing. Perhaps the candidates themselves were to blame, offering tired policies that failed to 'ignite' the voters? This seems unlikely. Beyond the three main parties, couch potatoes here in Exeter had a choice of UKIP, Green, Socialist Alliance or Independent Liberal. Surely one of these provided an alternative?

John Major – the only man to run away from the circus to become an accountant – once said "When my back's against the wall, I turn around and fight", but 40% of the electorate didn't even bother to do that. Instead, they settled themselves deeper into the cushions, thumbed the remote control, and voted for Big Brother, before turning in for the night. Their sleep, in all probability, was dreamless.

August 2001

WELLINGTON IN MOUTH DISEASE

Only a handful of people in Britain know the truth about the 2001 outbreak of foot and mouth disease, and they are keeping quiet. But with the passing of the months it becomes apparent that there is something nasty in the air.

Many of those involved in the crisis – vets, butchers, farmers, forestry-commission workers, coal importers, slaughter-men etc – are convinced that it was started deliberately; also, that MAFF knew about it in September 2000 at the latest. Hard facts are thin on the ground. Perhaps the truth will never emerge; but there are pointers.

In October 2000, MAFF contacted the Forestry Commission and various dealers in wooden pallets, specifically asking whether they had enough stocks available to deal with a contagious outbreak in the national herd. This enquiry – MAFF claimed – was 'merely routine'. But the last time they made such a request was in 1967, during the last outbreak. The story broke on Radio 4's Today programme. I know. I heard it. Within hours the BBC had sat on it.

Nick Brown – the Agriculture Minister in borrowed wellington boots – blamed Chinese takeaways for supplying pigswill to farmers, then back-tracked, admitting no evidence.

The source of the outbreak was apparently 'traced' to Mr Waugh's farm, Burnside, in Northumbria. Waugh, of course, was the perfect candidate, a 'little' man whose animal husbandry was medieval, with long-dead animals littering the fields. An easy target, easily in the frame.

The Northumberland Report (published in 1968 after

the '67 outbreak) concluded that infected animals should be slaughtered immediately, then buried on the farm without delay. Funeral pyres should never be used – they only spread the disease.

We now hear stories – again from vets and MAFF employees – of phials of the virus having gone missing from a MAFF lab in County Durham in late 2000. No evidence, so this must be treated cautiously but it is worryingly consistent with the general background of mistrust and hidden agendas.

The noble Lord Whitty (former trades union bod, whose ignorance of the countryside is matched only by his political ineptitude) met with farmers on 2nd August. His audience could only groan with disbelief as he told them that their own practices were to blame for the disease.

As for future outbreaks of the disease there will be no further Government compensation. The combination of New Labour and the European Union are destroying our farming industry, our ability to produce and control our own food production. Those who dismiss this as paranoia should remember the saying: "There's no smoke without fire". And only a few months ago our countryside was shrouded with plenty of it.

September 2001

REGIONAL GOVERNMENT VERY INTERESTING

Mention the words Regional Government and most peoples' eyes will glaze over, just before they start looking for the nearest exit. As a conversational gambit it ranks up there with: "God, you're looking old ".

Regional government, let's face it, is a crushing bore, and great camouflage for those wishing to make political changes behind the scenery without anybody noticing, or until it's too late to stop them.

Britain was once divided into the counties we all know, with councillors elected by local people who could go to them with local problems. That is now changing, thanks to the European Union. On the sly, Britain has now been divided into twelve Euro-Regions, administered by groups called Assemblies.

The South-West Regional Assembly, headed by a man named Chester Long, meets every three months in County Hall, Exeter; an alternative local government, running alongside the existing one, which it intends to supplant. Responsible for an area encompassing Penzance, Salisbury and Gloucester, this is the new South-West, run from its feudal castle in Exeter.

When Mr Long's predecessor, Chris Clarke, was asked by UKIP, "Does it worry you that nobody outside this room has ever heard of you?" he replied, "Does it matter?"

The Assemblies claim that taking power from London and 'devolving it to the regions' brings government closer to the people. Not true. A resident of Penzance or Gloucester 'administered' from Exeter, will lose local accountability and national government in London, a flat-footed attempt by Brussels to sideline Westminster and ultimately shut it down. There's nothing new in this. The Romans called it "divide and rule".

If Mr Long and his unelected colleagues succeed in sweeping away a democratic process evolved over a thousand years, our only consolation – and it's slight – is that they will come to realise that the wind blows colder on the crest of the hill than it does on the slopes.

September 2001

ROBIN COOK, TRADE FIGURES & DIGESTIVES

Robin Cook, former Foreign Secretary, was always a great admirer of the European Union and never missed an opportunity to extol its virtues. "Withdrawal from the EU will cost Britain millions of jobs," he parroted. "40% of our exports go to Europe. As members of the EU we have a louder voice."

It must have been the Foreign Office digestives. Britain runs a massive £175 billion trade deficit with the EU. When we pull out we will not get embroiled in a trade war. Why should we? The French will sell us their wine, the Germans their cars. Even Neil Kinnock admitted publicly that the EU would not 'retaliate' if we left.

As for inward investment, we are the No 1 choice in Europe – you'd never believe it, but business is booming. It all confirms the fears of a former French Minister. When asked why they wanted such awkward customers as the British in their club, he replied: "We didn't want Britain sitting off the shores of Europe like an aircraft carrier".

As for Mr Cook's export figures of 40%... they are like listening to a blind man who muddles his right with his left: it's very kind of him but you'd rather he hadn't bothered. The actual figure is somewhere around 20%, taking into account earnings like tourism, the City and those of our exports which only pass through the great container port of Rotterdam, en-route to the rest of the world.

Maybe this explains why his old enemy, Gordon Brown, had him pushed out of his job after the June election.

October 2001

24

A BUSTED FLUSH

John Major threw in his cards, turned to his stunned supporters. "Well…" he said, "We lost". Quietly he rose from the table and left.

Four years later, in June 2001, election poker came back to town. William Hague faced Mr Blair across the green baize, behind a rampart of £1 coins. The lights were dimmed, the cards were shuffled and dealt. Mr Hague scanned his hand, controlling his expression. His cards were incredible. The best. Withdrawal from the European Union. Four aces and a king of spades. Mr Hague tossed them onto the discard pile and looked straight at the dealer. "Five new cards."

Reality is never that straightforward, of course: Hague had a Conservative Party to keep united. But it was the very weakness of his message (In Europe but not run by Europe) and his failure to address Britain's crumbling public services, that caused his defeat.

Blair's 'New Model Army' was encamped on the summit of a political Everest – puritanical, battle-hardened, armed to the teeth. Hague's only chance of taking the mountain was to find a clear simple 'Big Idea', such as withdrawal from the EU, supported by 50% of the British people, who had reached that opinion *without* any political guidance from Westminster.

Surely it's not *that* difficult, is it?

October 2001

TIGGERS DON'T LIKE THE EU

When Eeyore – the old grey donkey – was bounced into the river, he did not ask, "Is this a Hearty Joke, or is it the Merest Accident?" Instead, he thought to himself, "It's wet, if you know what I mean".

The real world is less charming than Christopher Robin's, and far more ruthless. When somebody treads on your face, they mean business, and right now British farmers are on their backs and drifting, wondering what hit them. The answer is depressingly simple: our membership of the European Union.

Cornwall, one of the most deprived areas of the EU, is on its knees. Brussels cannot be blamed for the death of tin mining, nor the imminent demise of china clay, but the rest can be laid at their door. The fishing industry has become a virtual theme park, an adjunct to tourism, with livestock farming next for the chop. Whose turn next?

And in London nobody cares. When the EU – to their credit – granted Objective 1 funding for Cornwall, it required matching funds from Parliament. But New Labour, with virtually no seats in the South-West, failed to put up the money.

During the recent general election Jeremy Paxman interviewed Tim Yeo, the Tory agriculture spokesman, on BBC 2's Newsnight: "Come on, Mr Yeo, *nobody* enters politics to become Agriculture Minister..." Unfortunately Mr Paxman is probably right. In a nutshell, that is the fundamental problem.

It is not a hearty joke, nor the merest accident. It is deliberate policy. The Mafia have a saying: "Once is happenstance, twice is coincidence; the third time it's enemy action".

October 2001

TRIBUTE TO MIKE ROBERTSON

All of you who have followed this column will know that Tripehound, my father Mike, ceased writing it early this year as his health increasingly failed him.

Sadly he slipped away last Friday and the faithful old wide-carriage Imperial will be silent forever. In it still sits a last unfinished 'Leader' which maybe I'll have a crack at when things settle down. I'm sure he'd like that.

This was a man who started out as a Cadet on HMS Worcester, joined the Merchant service and later went to war as a Motor Transport Fitter in the RAF, where he met my mother Gina while on active service in Belgium. Her life ended shortly after I was born, and Mike already having tried his hand at dye casting, clothing manufacturing, making wallpaper printing machines, and the occasional decoy pigeon to name but a few ventures, decided to start a new life here in Polperro.

Between them, he and my late Stepmother Pam, built up a chain of cafes and restaurants which with a little extra income from the odd dabble in property and his beloved charter boat, Quesada, paid the school fees and kept the wolf from the door. But it was only after a chance conversation with a chap on the side of the road, that he found his true vocation, which of course was Trago.

We all need a little luck in life, and the secret is recognising yours when it comes along and grasping it with both hands. And Mike certainly did that. As many of you know, he retired shortly after Pam died in the mid '80s and moved to Ireland to start yet another new life with Sue and which I know brought them much happiness at Dromquinna, his paradise on the Kenmore River. To me he was the finest father, mentor, business partner and friend… whilst to others he may have appeared a bloody minded, mercurial and obstinate so-and-so. In reality he was a surprisingly shy and private person, extraordinarily generous and ultimately, as innately a decent man as I have ever had the privilege to know.

He is lost to us now, in body at least, but will be with us in spirit for as long as this column continues to run and which was his most fervent wish. Whether condemning the overcrowding on the Torpoint ferry or criticising Edward Heath over Europe, Tripehound got people thinking - irrespective of whether they agreed with him or not.

The column was his personal crusade for justice and increasingly in latter years a clarion call to its readers to wake up to the insidious threat of our involvement with the Great European Misadventure.

Continue it most certainly will now - and Mike and I will always be indebted to those stalwarts who have stepped into the breach and written so splendidly since the Spring. Thank you Rupert, David and Nina. I can think of no finer tribute to a wonderful life than to maintain this tradition that already spans more than 30 years.

Don't ask me for an epitaph as I suspect it will be unprintable, something to do with authority and two fingers. Let's just leave it that Mike's column may not have changed the world, but thank heavens the world never changed Mike. Amen to that. Take care Pop, wherever you are.

Bruce Robertson (aka Tripehound Pup)

15th November 2001

THE TRAIN LEAVING PLATFORM ONE...

The train prepared for departure. Doors slammed along its length. The Guard fingered his whistle and studied the hands of the station clock. The engines altered from tick-over to whine.

Nanny was starting to panic. Young Henry didn't seem to want to go. She'd packed his bags, said all the right words, got him to Waterloo in plenty of time. But now the boy's face was a mask.

"Nanny...I don't want to go"

"Don't be so silly, Henry. Everybody else is aboard... Porter, these cases. At once".

Henry pulled back. "But Nanny...why am I going?"

"Look lively now, Henry. The train will leave without you. Here, an empty compartment".

By now the boy was close to tears. "But Nanny...where am I going?"

"To Europe, young man. You'll love it there. Uncle Edward has arranged everything. Do try to stop snivelling, for heaven's sake, dear. And do remember to write!"

October 2001

For pedants or train-spotters: Young Henry would now, of course, be departing from St Pancras.

WRAPPING FISH BY TOMORROW

A certain Mr Coley from Cornwall, has criticised this column as xenophobic and racist, of raking up the last war and spreading "vile propaganda".

Confusingly, he also brought in homosexuality, though where that came from I have no idea. He also disagreed with Trago using its advertising space to support UKIP's call for total withdrawal from the European Union.

Firstly, criticising the EU is perfectly valid. Britain deserves at least one mainstream political party prepared to challenge this disastrous European experiment. If folks disagree with us, they can do so at election-time. Secondly, it is entirely justifiable to criticise German, French, Spanish etc... governments without being "racist". Or am I being "Anglophobic" when questioning my own government?

The crucial difference that has by-passed Mr Coley is that UKIP has no quarrel with the people of Europe, only with the arrogant elite manning the bridge of the EU super-tanker. If such criticism ever becomes illegal then we will have become so precious and repressed we'll have lost the thing that keeps us civilised: the ability to disagree without reaching for a gun. Isn't that how civil wars begin?

On the subject of Trago advertising, it is blindingly obvious to every reader – whatever their politics – that these views are from one side of the fence. The news media spreads a far more insidious message, wrapped up in the shiny paper of soap operas and light-entertainment. What I suspect Mr Coley dislikes is that Trago has the courage to lead from the front: an independent voice in a grey world of conformity, where keeping ones head down has now become the norm.

November 2001

POLITICIAN ADVISES AUSTRALIANS ON IMMIGRATION

When Ben Bradshaw was merely a Labour MP he could get away with crass remarks (on the abolition of the House of Lords: "It's time to sweep away the bigots and old farts") while his description of the low turnout at the general election as "An apathy of contentment" made the blood freeze. But his recent promotion to the Foreign Office will involve a crate of banana skins. Him heap big wrong man in wrong job.

On 4 September he wrote to the newspapers, praising East Timor for offering sanctuary to 400 of the Afghan refugees stranded aboard the Norwegian freighter 'Tampa', in stark contrast to the response from Australia, which didn't want them.

As a junior minister in the Foreign Office, Mr Bradshaw's opinions are important, and raise a number of issues, particularly as his letter was a coded criticism of Australia's policy on illegal immigration.

The government in Canberra provided food, medicine and medical staff for those aboard the vessel, but refused point-blank to allow them onto dry land. Mr Bradshaw, along with many other hopeless "progressives", called this shameful in his letter, though I suspect that governments throughout the world have a sneaking respect for Australia's actions. Majority opinion in Britain certainly bears this out.

The Australian people – including ethnic minorities who themselves had to jump through the bureaucratic hoops to gain citizenship – are 80% in support of their own government, whilst New Labour in Britain attracted only 25% of the vote at the general election, hardly a ringing endorsement. Even Neil Kinnock got more support when he lost to John Major in 1992.

A pattern begins to emerge. Faced with crisis, New Labour goes into ostrich-mode, revealing a fundamental incompetence, compounded by political correctness.

Their immigration policy has been an unmitigated disaster, with pitch invasions down the Channel tunnel and widespread social unrest because the numbers coming in are just too great.

Our public services are over-burdened enough as it is.

Any nation that tries to ethnically ring-fence itself will fall flat on its face. New blood and fresh ideas are vital. But genuine racial integration must be organic, gradual and properly managed; not based on chaos-theory and patronising references to tikka masala.

Many people from ethnic minorities in Britain, who have been here for generations, working hard, contributing to the nation and building up businesses, must be hanging their heads in despair, especially when anyone who sticks their head above the parapet gets it blown off, with the triumphant cry of 'racist!'

November 2001

GONE FISHING

Somebody once described a net as a collection of holes tied together with string (rather like the European Union's fishing policy, it seems to me). I am standing on Brixham quayside with my back to a fish and chip shop, gazing out across the harbour, awaiting the arrival of my companion. We are going fishing.

The town is packed with holidaymakers; good news for the traders. On a nearby bench, a seagull built like

Mussolini perches motionless, eying- up a discarded beef-burger. But the harbour itself - the reason why we are here, the reason why here exists at all - is almost empty, save for a handful of fishing boats. Not so long ago it was possible to cross the bay on foot, stepping from boat to boat. If I tried that today I'd get a soaking.

An industry has died here. The evidence is all around: the former fish-warehouses, net-makers and chandlers, the smoking-houses, rope-merchants and ice-houses; all gone. Even the hundreds of fishermen's cottages overlooking the harbour are occupied by those whose only connection with the sea is, for the most part, limited to a good view as they sit down to breakfast. The same story is repeated in ports all around Britain, from Grimsby to Penzance.

The tragedy is that most of this has happened over the last thirty years, since we joined the Common Market. Yet it was all so avoidable. Over-fishing and new technology played their part... one boat can now hoover up a week's catch in an afternoon...but when Edward Heath signed away our fishing grounds in the 1970's it was a tolling of the bell.

UK skippers could now sell their licences to foreign trawler-owners, and retire. And the truth is that many did; they could see the writing on the wall and knew that they were "politically insignificant" as Heath allegedly admitted to one of his colleagues in the 1970s.

As for the quota system, it has been an ecological disaster, with skippers throwing perfectly good fish back overboard, to sink to the seabed in a putrid decaying carpet.

The latest EU brainwave is to restrict the fishing of cod, allowing stocks to recover. But at the same time they have granted licences to fish for sand-eels, the main diet of cod. To quote Terry Wogan: "Is it me?"

It could all have been so different; the model lies across the North Sea in independent Norway. Free of the EU straitjacket they have maintained a thriving fishing industry, not the tourist theme park of ports like Brixham. My fishing companion has not shown up. With a heavy heart I collect my rods and drive home.

November 2001

10 GREEN BOTTLES

Radio 4 recently ran a report on climate change. Experts predict that one-third of humanity will be chronically short of water within fifty years. Massive irrigation projects will be needed to protect existing agricultural land, impacting on the environment: i.e. wetlands, marshes and river eco-systems.

The media often run scare-stories, but if this one is true we must ask why the European Union and New Labour are conspiring to destroy British livestock farming, particularly the smaller family farms. We have an established agricultural industry in this country, with generations of know-how, the perfect climate, and an ideal landscape. Once they are gone, they are gone forever. Rain we have in abundance. With global warming – to mangle New Labour's anthem – "Things ... can only get wetter".

The useful thing about cows and sheep is that when you position them on a hill they don't get flattened by bad weather or roll away like a tractor. But in their wisdom, our urban leaders have decided that livestock farming will move abroad. Britain will be dependent on foreign livestock imports, with no control over quality, animal husbandry or food safety.

Evidence of this is the recent discoveries of German and Dutch meat entering the UK, containing banned brain and spinal cord material. How many such consignments have already slipped through the net?

One by one, our own industries are being knocked off the wall like so many green bottles. Coal, steel, fishing, farming. Why are the British are so content to sit back as their country is wound up and asset-stripped beneath them by un-elected bureaucrats in Brussels?

December 2001

2002

A GRAND TOUR

Being xenophobic Little-Englanders we went down to Southern Italy for our holidays. The food was awful. No roast beef, no Yorkshire pud, no Spotted Dick, not even proper custard. But the Italians themselves were very pleasant, and Mrs Challice was particularly impressed with the punctuality of the trains.

Down in Puglia I engaged in conversation with a group of olive-growers, a cheerful bunch, happy with life. I didn't get to grips with the lingo, of course, but as I told them: "Your English is splendid. Well done!"

Over a few litres of wine in the local tavern we eventually got onto politics. I asked them: "What do you think about all those rules and regulations from Brussels?"

They looked at each other, and one of them smiled as he refilled my glass. "You mean the *English Laws*?"

"No, I mean all that bureaucracy from the European Union"

He set down the bottle. "Allow me to explain... We call them the English Laws because you're the only ones stupid enough to obey them." He gave a shrug and screwed his cigarette into the ashtray. "Here in Puglia no one takes any notice. We never did."

I left that tavern a wiser, if less sober, man.

January 2002

DENTISTRY AND...?

As an old man the poet, Sir John Betjeman, was once asked: "What are the main improvements you have seen during your lifetime?"

He thought for a moment, looked up from his wheelchair and gave a mischievous grin." I think possibly dentistry".

Betjeman had a point. A cultural revolution has taken place in Britain during the last forty years, a concerted attack against the pillars of the establishment: against the Church, the Monarchy, the Aristocracy, the Family. Our customs, manners, and standards of behaviour have been undermined and overwhelmed. Even raising the subject is considered bonkers in certain circles. How did we get here?

Journalist Peter Hitchens does not admire the 'progressives responsible. In his book The Abolition of Britain he writes: "This is the joy of being a progressive". Whenever your views are rejected by experience, common sense and tradition, it is because you are ahead of the rest of the population, never because you are eccentric or wrong, or just plain arrogant, or because they are not convinced by your arguments. They will catch up, and if not, so much the worse for them."

Arndale Centres are the new cathedrals, Posh and Becks the new aristocrats. Soap operas fill the void left by grandparents, while 'traditional' families are a dying trend. As for the Monarchy, we are effectively ruled by the European Union in Brussels, to whom the police and armed forces will soon have to swear allegiance. Even the name England has been regionalised and wiped from the map.

Somehow, incredibly, we let this happen before our eyes. Sedated by bread and circuses, by that magic box in the corner of the sitting room, we surrendered the very things that made us what we were. It is all very strange.

January 2002

LIVING ON AN ISLAND

A chap called Ivan Hall recently wrote to the newspapers suggesting that UKIP and other like-minded 'Europhobes' should all disappear to the Isle of Wight and leave sensible people like him to get on with their lives in the 21st Century.

What a brilliant idea, Ivan. When you get your scheme up and running, please send me a couple of passports. It'll be a haven. An island free of litter, with schools where children (not 'clients') are taught subjects they'll actually find useful in later life; where hospitals have the money to treat patients properly, not leave them defecating on trolleys in the corridor; where the police are freed from the handcuffs of political correctness and left to get on with the job of keeping the peace; an island where business people are valued as wealth-generators, not tied hand and foot by petty regulations and idiotic bureaucracy; an island where a telephone call actually results in talking to a real human being, and where failure and corruption in high places are punished...not rewarded by golden handshakes.

There will be other advantages. Unlike Britain, we could always have an immigration policy, not the mess we're currently saddled with. On agriculture, we can enjoy fresh, home-grown organic food, uncontaminated by dodgy GM technology and factory-scale use of antibiotics.

As for our defence force, at least they will know who they are defending, and why. Six rowing boats and two bi-planes should be enough. Presumably Mr Hall and his chums will be very happy on the mainland, basking in their membership of the EU's Soviet-style utopia, so no threat of invasion there.

And the best of luck to you, Mr Hall. If it all goes horribly wrong, which it probably will, at least we tried to warn you. The only problem I can foresee is 'overpopulation'. At a rough estimate, forty million Britons will want to take up residence there, hence our early application for passports... (We'd like to grab a decent property before the rush.)

April 2002

A GRAND TRADITION

The British have a great tradition of taking their defeats and somehow, incredibly, turning them into victories, a tradition which leaves outsiders shaking their heads in genuine bewilderment.

A few examples from history: the Saxon King, Alfred the Great, is known to millions not because he eventually tamed the Danes but because, dejected and on the run, he fell asleep over an old lady's cakes and let them burn on the fire. For this, quite rightly, his ears were boxed, earning him a permanent place in the historical record.

The Battle of Hastings is marked by the one date that almost everyone educated in Britain can reel off at the drop of a hat: 1066...when the French won.

Perhaps our greatest victory/defeat (with the possible exception of 'Scott of the Antarctic') occurred during the

Crimean War, when the Light Brigade charged the wrong guns in the wrong valley, and were blown to smithereens. We were very fond of this one, and even wrote a poem about it.

There are more recent examples: in 1940, the German Army trod all over us in France, chasing us onto the beach at Dunkirk, from where we only escaped complete disaster by the people of Britain taking a hand, chugging across the Channel in their pleasure boats to rescue the trapped soldiers, though it's only fair to point out that Winston Churchill was under no illusions, pointing out to everybody who would listen: "Wars are not won by evacuations"

Britain now faces an equally serious threat... and "no," this is not anti-German, or anti-anybody else for that matter, the European Union excepted, of course. The battle of the EU Constitution is hugely important, as Tony Blair is well aware, and if we lose it there will be no question of cheering ourselves up afterwards with talk of victory/defeats.

April 2002

FRIDGE MAGNETISM

Residents in Exeter are trying to block plans for a dump of unwanted fridges in the heart of the City. The result will be a potential death-trap for children, a threat to passing intercity trains, and an eyesore to everyone in the area.

The "Fridge Mountain" is another piece of the EU jigsaw (along with those dumped cars littering our roadsides: windscreens smashed, burnt-out, and trashed). What a metaphor. What a glorious monument to the Kafka-like bureaucracy in Brussels, and to a British Government that, quite clearly, cares more about implementing EU directives than its own national welfare.

The Minister holding the bomb when the music stopped was Michael Meacher. He feinted to the left, sold everyone a dummy and tossed the bomb back to Brussels. Interviewed by an incredulous BBC journalist Mr Meacher explained what had gone wrong: "We wrote to the EU nine times, asking for clarification, but they never wrote back to us"

Surely it's not beyond even the most EU-loving politician to have enough gumption to tell Brussels: "Sorry, we got it wrong on the fridges. Didn't read the small print. We'll bring these rules into effect but only when we've established a nationwide system of disposal". That would have been a proper government, putting its own people before the EU, not behaving like a performing poodle on a trampoline: "Is this high enough? I can go higher...Just watch."

This is a taster, just a taster, of what British business has endured for the last 30 years, a blizzard of useless regulations from the EU, (30,000 of them at the last count). With none of them, not a single one, ever having been repealed.

April 2002

This was another campaign that worked, a joint effort between UKIP and Yolanda Henson, the local Conservative Councillor who worked her socks off... In marked contrast to the Lib Dem who was in favour of Fridge Central (In the ensuing local election Henson easily won)

MORE NITTY GRITTY

It is now official: you may not use the term "Nitty Gritty", due to its connotations of Racism, and you certainly wouldn't want to be accused of that. The word "Jazz", for reasons which escape me, is also highly suspect, so it's probably best avoided.

Eskimos are now the "Inuit", Red Indians are "Native Americans", and Siamese twins are "co-joined", to avoid offending those citizens of Thailand who, some time in the distant future, might revert to calling their country Siam. It's useful to plan ahead with these things.

You may not have a brainstorming session. This is offensive to those with head-injuries. Use "Cloud-bursting" instead. Neither may you refer to a blindfold, for similar reasons. "Sight-shield" is better, more descriptive, and offends no one (at the moment, at least, but we will notify you of any changes).

An accident black-spot, is now, of course, a "Hot-spot"...and not before time, we think you'll agree. French Socialists, smashing restaurant windows and overturning cars in the centre of Paris because their man was eliminated in a free democratic election, are officially "Protesters", not rioters. Please try to remember that.

The above list is not exhaustive: for example, the wearing of Remembrance Day poppies is "Confusing to foreign visitors" and banned by certain visionary officials in the BBC, so bear that in mind next year.

Later in the calendar, it's worth remembering that "Father Christmas" is both sexist and elitist, imposing fixed roles and out-dated sexual stereotyping on society, in much the same way that the term "British" is "Potentially Racist" to anybody who has chosen to leave their own country and settle here.

Has Britain lost its mind, or did I just fall asleep and wake up in a parallel universe? Quite likely. But in case you're wondering, "Nitty Gritty" is apparently the detritus found in the bilges of a slave ship.

July 2002

IN THE BEAR... NOT EATEN BY THE BEAR

"I believe the days of the small farmer working on his own are numbered": the words of Lord Whitty, 19.01.02. So, not much cheer there then. And he's probably right. Whilst we stay in the EU our farming policy is decided in Brussels not in London.

Given their track record (an apprenticeship in the fishing industry, anyone?) it's no reason to hang out the flags. New Labour are making a big thing about the Curry Report, their cunning plan to solve the "problem" of British agriculture. In fairness, parts of this plan are quite good, but it has one huge flaw: our membership of the EU itself, and particularly of the Common Agricultural Policy. The CAP is a mess, and everyone agrees that (except the French, with thousands of peasant farmers, who do swimmingly well out of it and will never agree to changes, particularly after Le Pen ... the whole deal was that the Germans would get the banking and the French would get the farms and vineyards etc).

New Labour's weapon in the coming battle, the Curry Report, will prove to be as much use as a spud-gun. The report cannot even be considered before 2006 and is merely "aspirational". In other words, "We'd like to do it if we get the chance, but we probably won't, so don't get your hopes up".

Even worse, reforming the CAP is virtually impossible. Look at a few Tory manifesto-pledges down the years.

1979: **"We believe that radical changes in the operation of the CAP are necessary".**

1987: **"We seek a radical overhaul of the CAP".**

1992: **"We will re-double our efforts to reform the CAP".**

1997: **"We will continue to push for fundamental reform of the CAP".**

And if the Tories can't do it, Labour certainly won't.

July 2002

SOIL AND COMMON SENSE COMPOSTING

Organic farming in the rest of the EU grew by 25% in the last 10 years. In the UK it grew by half of 1%. As a result, we now import 70% of our organic food, most of which comes from Europe and could easily be grown here. This is not some sepia-tinted rural idyll, punctuated by the ticking of a farmhouse clock (nice as it sounds). This is a real opportunity to support an industry crying out for growth.

The money will come from the £4 billion we currently throw into the black hole of the CAP every year. Half of the EU's total annual budget, goes into the CAP, much of it on scams and fraud and on paying farmers to grow crops such as linseed which are then ploughed back into the land because it was never wanted in the first place and to harvest it would flood the market and kill the price.

We deserve good healthy food, not smothered in pesticides, or pumped full of steroids and antibiotics. Our food should be produced by local farmers who get paid a fair rate for their efforts, and if that means making it easier for them to hire staff (organic farming is labour-intensive) so be it. New Labour would disagree. In 1999 they spent £52 million on developing GM crops, and £13 million on improving the image of firms like Monsanto. That same year they spent £1.7 million on organic farming.

A quote from Graham Harvey's book, The Killing of the Countryside: "The most striking feature is the silence. There is no sound in this rolling prairie land; no buzzing of bees, no rasping of crickets, no birdsong...Down below the opening ears, on the bare earth, no bugs or insects are visible among the forest of stems. Nothing lives here; the pesticides have seen to that...Along with the invertebrates have gone the small mammals which lived on them. Finding a shrew or fieldmouse in this miserable monoculture is worth a letter to the Times".

Locked into the corruption and inefficiency of the EU, we are poisoning our land, and paying vast sums to Brussels as we do it. Meanwhile the exodus continues, with small family farms auctioned off to the Second Homers in London. What a state we're in.

August 2002

MINT SAUCE

The Shepherd tamped down the tobacco in his pipe, and ran an experienced eye across the hillside, checking his sheep and his newest dog. A gleaming 4x4 hurtled into view, bouncing across the field, wheels spinning on the damp grass. It parked near the Shepherd, and the driver got out: a young man in a suit of impeccable cut: the glasses were "aviator", the tie "Ramone", the Wellingtons spotless.

The apparition spoke. "Hi... Listen, if I tell you how many sheep you have in this flock, will you give me one?"

The Shepherd rattled his matches, thinking it over. "Why not?"

The driver punched a code into his cell-phone, surfed to the NASA web site, locked on to a GPS Satellite and, with a flourish, printed off a report. "You have..." he announced, "...1,647 sheep".

"True". The Shepherd lit his pipe. "So you win".

Gucci Wellingtons grabbed hold of his prize and bundled it into the back of the 4x4.

Then the Shepherd said, "Now it's my turn. Do I get that animal back if I can guess who you work for?"

"Sure...No problemo."

"You work," said the Shepherd, "for the European Union, and I'll tell you how I know. You turned up here without an invite, you expect payment for telling me something I already know, and you are clueless about farming because that's my dog in the back of your car".

August 2002

SHOOTING THE RAPIDS

Whenever Napoleon Bonaparte saw a trooper he didn't recognise he always fired three questions at him, in exactly the same order: "How old are you? How long have you been serving? Did you serve in either of my last two campaigns?"

A young Swedish recruit, not a French-speaker, was coached by his colleagues how to reply. But when Napoleon spotted him, for once he put the questions in the wrong order.

"How long have you been serving?" he asked the young Swede.

"Twenty three years, Excellency".

"Tiens!" exclaimed Napoleon. "Then... how old are you?"

"Three years".

"Sacre Tonnerre!" cried Napoleon, "either you are mad or I am".

"Both", said the Swede.

Which shows the importance of making oneself understood, and why the EU is doomed because of its lack of a common language.

A quick example of this: a couple of years ago the EU was debating a proposal when a delegate warned that they would be, "Shooting the rapids". The next speaker rose to his feet and began talking about animal welfare, totally unconnected with the subject. Labour MEPs looked at the Tories: the Lib-Dems looked at the UKIP. And everybody looked at everybody else, exchanging mystified looks. What was this man on about?

The debate meandered off for twenty minutes, before somebody asked: "Why are we all talking about animal rights?" It transpired that someone had mistranslated "Rapids" into "Shooting the Rabbits".

Every day in Brussels some 800 interpreters (backed up by 2,000 part-timers) attend meetings, conferences and social functions. At most conferences six languages operate, with two booths containing three interpreters each. Confused? They will be...because when the EU enlarges they will have 23 languages in operation, meaning 506 possible combinations. Do the words "Tower" and "Babel" come to mind? Look at the Strasbourg Parliament building and there it is in front of you. An exact replica, as they publicly admit.

August 2002

BAN ALL CARS

Before he became Mayor of London, Ken Livingstone said in 1999: "I hate cars. If I ever get any powers again I'd ban the lot". Ben Bradshaw, MP, obviously from the same stable, waved his cycle-clips in the air at a "Car-Free" day in Guildhall Shopping Centre and announced: "We need to make driving a car as anti-social as smoking". Presumably it never occurred to him that residents of, say, Sheepwash might find it rather difficult puffing to work on a bicycle.

These politicians are trying to un-invent the wheel. Thanks to Dr Beeching, who butchered our rail network in the 1960's, the main method of travel in today's Britain is the car, not the bicycle. Perhaps it's a tragedy, but it's also a fact. John Betjeman, in a wonderful old black-and-white documentary about Northlew, with untroubled cows mooching along a lane in high summer, said in 1960: "Traffic changes everything", and he was right. Once a lifestyle has changed, it's gone forever. We now live in a 7-Day a week world, rushing around like rats in a maze.

The war against the motorist has many fronts; all of them involve taking money from the individual and handing it to the State. This is a policy of creating traffic jams, in a doomed attempt to force people onto dirty, unreliable, and expensive public transport...let's not even mention Railtrack. Policemen, 'radar-zapping' motorists on dual carriageways travelling at 80mph in perfect safety. Useless bus-lanes that lie empty most of the time, clogging up the traffic, condemning everyone else to crawl along in low gear, pumping out pollution as their stress levels go through the roof, (when did "Road-Rage" enter our vocabulary?); all of which costs the local economy a fortune.

We all know that tail-gating somebody at 100mph in the outside lane of the motorway, whilst fumbling for that sandwich we dropped under the seat, should result in a lengthy ban. But there are limits to this. Like it or not, the car (and the lorry) are here to stay. A quick statistic... a Boeing 747, flying one-way from London to New York, creates more pollution than 40,000 cars travelling from London to Leeds and back again, yet there is no VAT on aviation fuel.

September 2002

NEARLY COMING TRUE

When Aldous Huxley wrote Brave New World in 1932, the philosopher Bertrand Russell commented: "It is all too likely to come true". Perhaps we're not there yet, but it's coming. Just give it a few more years.

"Bernard", the main character, wants to take Lenina walking in the Lake District, to have a chat with her away from the city...But Lenina is not so sure: walking and talking in the Brave New World seems a very odd way of spending an afternoon. Instead, she persuades him to fly them to Amsterdam to see the Women's Heavyweight Wrestling Championship (semi-finals).

Once he gets there, Bernard is a bit of a misery, not talking to her friends and declining the half-gramme raspberry-sundae (laced with soma, the State's own narcotic, designed to zonk out the populace...Much like 'Eastenders' today). "I'd rather be myself", he tells her. "Myself and nasty. Not somebody else, however jolly."

"A gramme in time saves nine," says Lenina. When Bernard impatiently pushes the glass away, she adds, "One cubic centimetre cures ten gloomy sentiments"; and when he tells her to shut up she's ready with another scrap of sleep-inducted wisdom: "A gramme is always better than a damn," and guzzles the sundae herself.

Travelling back over the English Channel in Bernard's helicopter (...this reminded me of the way Britain is "harmonising" with the EU...) the girl is so horrified by the sight of the pale face of the moon and the heaving, black foam-flecked water, the rushing emptiness of the night, that she desperately scrabbles for the equivalent of Radio 1, seeking the comfort of a reassuring voice, the voice of the State, telling her that everything will be alright.

Bernard switches off the radio. "I want to look at the sea in peace. It makes me feel as though...as though I were more me, if you see what I mean. More on my own, not so completely a part of something else. Not just a cell in a social body. Doesn't it make you feel like that, Lenina?"

To gain the full horror of Brave New World one should read the book. But the resonance is of a ruling class so convinced that it's "right" (and so all-powerful) that it doesn't even meet criticism with intellectual arguments. Instead it greets critics with a total and genuine lack of comprehension, a sort of wall-eyed, slack-mouthed stare, just like those in Britain today so embarrassed by their own country they can't wait to hand it over to the European Union, lock, stock, and barrel.

September 2002

IT'S NOT ALL BAD

Ben Bradshaw, MP, recently pointed out that we should thank the European Union for imposing hygiene-standards on drinking water in this country, and how we wouldn't have it if it weren't for our membership of the EU. This is an important point, going to the heart of things.

Only a fool would say that everything that comes from Brussels is stupid or wrong. There are some good things out there: one small example is that when you buy a kettle or an iron, it now comes with a plug attached; this makes good sense, and prevents the "electrically challenged" from plugging themselves into the National Grid. Certain aspects of Health & Safety law, not to mention employment legislation, are also welcome. But the crucial point...as Mr Bradshaw himself admitted with an almost despairing tone...is that past British governments should have brought in these things, but didn't.

My point is that the fact that they didn't is more a reflection on the unimaginative politicians we've had during the last thirty years, and less a glowing report on the merits of the EU. Mr Bradshaw's sub-text, and of others who toe the same line, is that British politicians can't be trusted to do things, so let's get 'Europe' to run it for us.

What a bunch of no-hopers. Politicians need the self-confidence to sort out things in their own bailiwick, not rely on outsiders to do it for them; that's why they're paid.

I'm not saying that British is always best (I cite the Millennium Dome, and the Austin Allegro) but where do we get this supine attitude that if it's from Europe (suave, sophisticated and cultured, in marked contrast to the clod-hopping English) then it must inevitably be better? This country is being led by people who have not only abandoned the bridge...They're on another ship.

October 2002

A BIT OF PAPER WITH THE QUEEN'S HEAD ON

The issue of the euro has split our country in a way we haven't seen for years. And opposition to it is deepening and strengthening. In desperation, the Yes campaign is using tired old insults of xenophobia and narrow-mindedness, neither of which get them anywhere. After all, nobody in their right mind would call Sir Bob Geldof a "Little Englander".

This is not about a bit of paper with the Queen's head

on it. If we join the euro, the Chancellor of the Exchequer will no longer control UK interest rates, taxation or public spending. They'll be controlled by the European Bank. It's called "one size fits all" and it doesn't work, anymore than assuming that a single pair of trousers will fit everyone in the room.

The "Yes" refer to the "over-valued" pound. But this is muddled thinking. The pound is not over-valued. The pound is valued sixty times a minute by currency traders around the world. The pound's 'value' is only what someone will pay for it at the time. A clapped out Ford Escort with no MOT is worth less than one in the showroom. As with cars, so with currencies. The buyer, not the seller, determines the price.

October 2002

POOP, POOP... MAKE WAY FOR THE MARVELOUS MR TOAD

A certain Mr Clemence has objected to my recent comments about traffic cops "radar zapping people travelling on dual-carriageways at 80mph in perfect safety". He felt that the UK Independence Party had been the only party worth voting for, but now this was gone for him, and it was all my fault.

I apologise if I offended Mr Clemence, and hope he reconsiders his decision not to participate in future elections, but I'm afraid that I stick to my guns on this one.

Any motorist who screams past a school with smoke coming from their tyres should be banned, and we've all seen idiots overtaking on blind bends, tail-gating on motorways, and generally not giving a damn about their fellow road-users. But we're not talking about that. This is about big wide roads and drivers at the wheel of modern cars equipped with ABS, traction control, and many other safety features.

Good driving consists of knowing your vehicle, adjusting to local conditions, using mirrors and indicators, judging the "mood" of the traffic, the creation of an invisible "safety buffer" around you, and the ability to predict what other drivers are about to do, and take evasive action before they do it.

In the right conditions, 80mph on a dry motorway, with good visibility, and an alert, competent driver, is very safe. And if Mr Clemence still doesn't believe me, I invite him to try pootling up the M5 at 60mph, and he'll soon find his rear-view mirror filling up with 44 tonnes of truck or National Express coach; so close, in fact, that he'll be able to reach backwards and pluck that Yorkie bar from the driver's breast pocket.

October 2002

...AND MONTMORENCY TOO

In "Three Men in a Boat" Jerome K Jerome describes the pool under Sandford lasher: "(the pool), just behind the lock, is a very good place to drown yourself in. The undercurrent is terribly strong and if you once get down into it you are all right. An obelisk marks the spot where two men have already been drowned, while bathing there; and the steps of the obelisk are generally used as a diving board by young men who now wish to see if the place really is dangerous".

There is a parallel here. The Irish, by voting yes to the Nice Treaty, have just jumped into the pool under

Sandford lasher. Nobody can say they weren't warned'; the obelisk was up, the notices posted and when Eire goes under for the third time, she can blame only herself. The problem is that she will drag us down with her.

The Nice Treaty allows the European Union to "enlarge" to take in a further ten countries (Poland, Latvia, Estonia etc). These nations are an odd mix. Some are economic basket-cases and we'll be digging deeper into our pockets to bale them out. Proof of this is that when Germany took East Germany under its wing, the nation went from economic tiger to comparative pussycat in ten years.

Some of the other countries (Latvia and Estonia in particular) are thriving, vibrant, forward looking and are now having second thoughts about joining the EU. They recognise that once the dead hand of Brussels has fallen across the tiller, they will have given up control of their own affairs and after years of Soviet-dominated bullying perhaps they'd be better off running their own show rather than swapping one distant master in Moscow for another one in Belgium.

As for the Irish, do they realise what they've done? Probably not. Do they care? Well, if not now, in a few years they certainly will. We all will.

November 2002

WHO'S HE THEN?

John Major once said: "When my back's against the wall, I turn around and fight". Well the Tories are doing it again. To mangle Monty Python: "When danger reared its ugly head, they bravely turned their tail and fled".

At the recent Conservative Party Conference, the new leader Mr Duncan-Smith warned his Party not to "underestimate the determination of a quiet man". But he's not just 'quiet': he's inaudible. Show his photograph to people in the street and they'll shake their heads: "Nope. Seen him somewhere, but no idea"

The Tories lost in 1997. Sleaze, VAT on fuel, and Poll Tax played their part but the main cause was 'Europe'. When we joined the ERM (forerunner of the euro) we ran smack into recession. Unemployment soared, along with interest rates; homes were repossessed and we were all introduced to the phrase 'negative equity'. We even had businessmen plonking the keys to the premises onto the bank manager's desk with the words: "Here... you try running it. At these rates, I can't".

The Western Morning News ran a readers' poll on the euro back in February 2002.

JOIN THE EURO?

Now..107

When conditions are right............146

Never..5444

A total rejection rate of 95.55%. If Tony Blair, from his own Party Conference speech, wishes to be BOLD that's his prerogative, but he should remember the old saying: "There are old pilots and there are bold pilots. But there are no old, bold pilots". Iraq, PFI, the euro. Can you smell burning? It's that man again, flying too close to the sun.

November 2002

YANKEE DOODLE DANDEE

During the last few years UKIP and others have warned that Britain is being dragged deeper into the European Union, without the knowledge or permission of the British People. Critics rubbish this, with insults like "small-minded" or "anti-European". But their problem is that when sat upon, the truth has an uncanny way of biting back, just where it's least welcome.

This one is very simple. The EU is now drawing up a constitution for itself, because it wants to "reconnect" with the voters of Europe. But they are going about it in a very odd way. Their Convention on the Future of Europe has been "tasked" with the job, and seems likely to introduce an "exit clause", making it virtually impossible for Britain to leave the EU.

If these proposals go through, any state wishing to withdraw will need the backing of three-quarters of the votes in the EU Council of Ministers, two-thirds of the votes of the EU Parliament, and ratification by the parliament of every single member-country, before they are allowed to leave. This is the clanging of the cell door, the final turn of the key.

This brilliant idea was presented by Andrew Duff, MEP, chief draftsman of the European Liberals, who went on to explain why he'd done it: "We don't want to end up like the USA when the South wanted to leave and the North had to fight to keep them in". (The American Civil War resulted in the slaughter of 700,000 men, and the maiming of a further 500,000).

I can't speak for you, but I'm a bit worried about Mr Duff. He seems to think that the interests of the EU come before those of British voters, and if we leave the EU then it might lead to a war. If this is true, are they even the sort of people we should be doing business with? To avoid this, Mr Duff wants to lock us in for ever. Whose side is he on?

November 2002

STICKS & STONES

Words are important things. And when others try to gag you then it becomes mind control and no joke. Political correctness is intrusive, patronising, and insulting... In schools a blackboard is now a 'chalkboard', black pudding is 'breakfast pudding' and British history, if it's taught at all, is given a PC spin. It is also fascinating that the old system of 'houses' on the sports field has gone. The cultural Marxists in charge of our children's education don't want them to realise that people sometimes lose. The phrase 'egg and spoon race' might plunge them into trauma in later life.

A more recent victim was Robin Page, the Telegraph journalist, former presenter of One Man & His Dog, and a passionate supporter of country life. On 6 Sept, at a rally in Gloucestershire, Mr Page encouraged his audience to attend the Countryside March: these are his own words: "I urged that the rural minority be given the same legal protection as other minorities. All I said was that (they) should have the same rights as blacks, gays and Muslims...What is wrong with that in a multicultural society?"

Somebody obviously disagreed. Mr Page was asked to attend a police interview near his Cambridge farm. When he refused to answer questions without his lawyer present, he was arrested and spent 40 minutes in a police cell. He was then told that he'd spend the night there if he remained silent, and was then quizzed as to whether he was a racist... And remember, this happened in Britain.

As Mr Page said: "Whereas once you were innocent until proven guilty, Gloucestershire police now assume you are guilty until proven innocent. It seems to me that I'm being stitched up by the anti-hunting lobby and the politically correct."

November 2002

WHERE IT ALL WENT WRONG

King George V was travelling in the back of a car with Sir Anthony Blunt (who, among other things, was a very dedicated Russian agent) gazing out on the wooded banks of the River Thames, when he observed that they were passing the Isle of Runnymede, site of the signing of the Magna Charta in 1215. The King, who probably wouldn't have recognised a Russian spy if they'd walked up to him waving a red flag, turned to Blunt and said: "That's where everything started to go wrong".

From George's point of view he was right. The signing of the Magna Charta was the beginning of democracy in this country, and the end of the monarch's divine right to rule. (The barons effectively turned around to their king and said: "No...You're not a god, and your people have rights, too", and forced him to sign a document confirming it), though it has to be admitted that a few hundred years later Sir Thomas More lost his head in a similar quarrel with Henry VIII. These things take time to work themselves out.

From Magna Charta (who probably died in vain)

through to Cromwell, and Emmeline Pankhurst's suffragettes throwing themselves in front of racehorses, people have fought for their right to vote. But now, most people view politics with disdain or cynical amusement. "Why vote? They're all the same".

The low turnout at the last election (60%) means that Tony Blair's New Labour clones attracted only 25% of the vote. But the politicians don't care about low turnout; as long as they get more votes than the other lot. If we just stay at home they will dismiss that as an "apathy of contentment" to quote Jack Straw the other day.

December 2002

THE TWELTH DAY OF CHRISTMAS THE EU SENT TO ME...

Dearest Commissioner Kinnock,

The twelve leaping lords were a very kind thought, but with great regret I must decline them. They have proved to be so disruptive about the house, vaulting over the children, not taking "No" for an answer, and generally creating havoc... And aren't Lords terribly "last century" in Europe? In Britain, we're no longer allowed them.

The eleven ladies dancing were, however, most welcome and will certainly prove a diversion for some of the gentlemen here; though with the ten pipers piping and nine drummers drumming, I fear that things may get a little crowded in the hall, and am therefore returning the latter two with thanks. I enclose the bill they have passed me for their expenses.

I have at last contacted the French Ambassador, who, in a spirit of true 'entente cordiale', has kindly agreed to take on the eight maids a-milking. You'll understand that we no longer milk cows in this country, so the gift, however well meant, was a little... how may I put it? ...redundant.

The seven birds were a great excitement, but upon closer scrutiny proved to be ugly ducklings. How strange: the EU paperwork clearly describes them as swimming swans. Perhaps you could look into this; I'd be most grateful: the village pond looks so empty just now.

At first sight the six geese-a-laying were more successful. But they just won't STOP laying, and we are now way, way over quota. We have a mountain of eggs and I simply don't know what to do with them all. You're such a sensible dear. Surely you can come up with something? Everyone here would be so grateful.

My Dear Neil... or should I now use your official title of "Anti-Corruption Supremo"? I'm shocked. **Five gold rings**? Surely one would have been sufficient? We will never speak of this again.

The four colly birds (hereabouts we call them blackbirds) were doubtless well intentioned but feelings still run high on the subject of subsidised coal from the EU and all those job losses in Wales and further afield; and people can be so tiresome in the associations they make. I know you'll understand if I return them with the pipers, the lords, etc... (This sounds dreadfully ungrateful, I know, but you've always been so stern about "transparency", and after your recent 'contretemps' with that accountant woman, Andreasen, and her horrid accusations... Well, it's probably for the best).

The three French hens are similarly contentious. Battery farming is apparently under threat in the UK though not in the rest of Europe, which has gone down badly in the local area. And these particular hens do *rather seem* to have had a hard life. Taking everything into consideration I am despatching them by Eurostar. Perhaps you could alert your dear wife that they are en-route?

The two turtledoves were delicious though, as was the partridge, and you'll be pleased to know that the pear tree is making a roaring blaze even as I write

December 2002

2003

URBAN REGENERATION

"Exeter was a jewel", said Hitler, "We have destroyed it". But the City Council could have taught even the Luftwaffe a trick or two on urban planning when they bulldozed huge areas that had largely escaped the bombing, the irreplaceable parts of Old Exeter, now gone forever: Sidwell Street, the Theatre Royal; even Bedford Circus... rivalling anything in Bath... could have been salvaged and rebuilt.

Instead, the whole lot came down in a cloud of dust and rubble. What contempt for the past; what criminal lack of taste. Instead we had the Orwellian drabness of post-war Exeter. For those who knew it before, it must have been heart-rending to see such vandalism visited upon their once-beautiful city.

The battle continues. This time it's down on the quay. Exeter City Council intends to "improve" and "regenerate" the area. This means gated apartments and two public information boards: "You are now standing where the Chandler's used to be."

All those scruffy boats will have to go. We can't have people doing real things with pots of paint and screwdrivers, making all sorts of mess. Sends out the wrong signal.

The boat-owners and small traders, the one-man-bands in their workshops on the quayside, are all in the path of this juggernaut. But without the traders, the rowing club, and the boat-owners, the quay will be sterile; a litter-strewn wilderness overlooked by security gates, cameras and razor-wire. This part of

Exeter is a genuine, working link with the past. We don't need to dress hired extras in costumes for the benefit of school-parties. The real thing is here already, and our myopic Council - as blind as ever - wants to sweep it away.

They have offered the boat-owners another site, on a reclaimed waste tip, with unstable subsoil, (How can a crane hoist up a boat if three of its legs are sinking into mush?) with electric power-lines crackling overhead, inflammable gases present in the soil, no security from thieves or vandals, a restriction on larger vessels, and no ancillary buildings; all immediately downwind of a meat rendering plant renowned for the vile fumes it pumps out, so noxious that you have to cover your face as you walk past.

I have a better idea. Why doesn't the Council concentrate on cleaning up the rest of the city before wrecking one of the few remaining pieces of Exeter that are a real link with the past? They could even apply to Brussels for a grant, and get some of our cash back into this country, right where it belongs.

January 2003

The protest (which included this article) worked surprisingly well. At the time of writing, the boatyard is still there, scruffy as ever.

OLLIE NORTH

America, 1987, and Lt. Col Oliver (Ollie) North is testifying to the Iran-Contra enquiry, a scandal which is threatening to bring down President Ronald Reagan. A senator begins the questioning, with one eye on getting a laugh from his audience: "Did you not recently spend $60,000 on a home security system...? Isn't that a little excessive?"

"No Sir", replied North, "The lives of my family and I were threatened by a terrorist."

The senator regarded North with a cool gaze. "What terrorist could possibly scare you that much?"

"His name is Abu Nidal, Sir", said North… "He is the most evil person alive that I know of. If it was up to me, I would recommend that an assassin team be formed to eliminate him and his men from the face of the earth."

The senator disagreed with this and passed on to another subject. Abu Nidal, you may be interested to know, was a Libyan terrorist leader, forerunner of Osama Bin Laden.

One year earlier to Ollie North's evidence, in 1986, terrorist Mohammed Atta was jailed for blowing up a bus in Israel. As part of the Oslo Peace Agreement in 1993 the Israelis had agreed to release Palestinian "political prisoners" but they flatly refused to release any killers, one of whom was Atta. Enter the U.S. President, Bill Clinton, who insisted that ALL prisoners be released, regardless. The Israelis, shaking their heads at such incredible naivety, threw open the jails and the Arab terrorists hit the streets.

If the name Mohammed Atta sounds familiar he was one of the pilots who later flew an airliner into Tower One of the World Trade Centre on 11 September… That's what happens when you go soft on terrorists. Once you've outlived your usefulness, they bite off your arm.

January 2003

This piece was based on a fairly well known email circulating at the time. In one version Abu Nidal was even replaced by Osama Bin Laden, which would have made it to the front pages, if true.

A PLUCKY BRITISH 'DO'

In a recent letter to 'This England' magazine a correspondent explained the ups and downs of obtaining a replacement driving-licence not plastered in EU symbols. Having changed address, he sent away his licence. The DVLA wrote back, saying that they needed a passport-sized photo before they could issue the new document.

Our hero, and that's what he is, noticed that the paperwork showed the EU banner but no British flag. As he explained to them, he considered himself 'British' and not 'European' so please could he have his old licence back? No, explained DVLA, he was stuck with a new licence, but if he gave them a call they could discuss it on the telephone.

To quote his letter: "I asked if I could put a small Union Jack above my shoulder in the photo, and was told they would 'edit it out'. So I asked if I could put it on my shirt, high up on the chest. Again I was told that they would 'edit it out'. By now I felt I was being told that I could not be British, so I asked what they would do if I had a Union Jack tattooed on my forehead? This they could not answer immediately, but later they rang back and, much to my surprise, agreed. So I stuck a small Union Jack onto my forehead with sellotape and sent off the photograph. As you can see, I received my licence. I may look a bit odd to some people but I feel good because I took on the red-tape brigade, and won!"

And if you read that man's letter with a smile of sneering contempt, may I suggest that you acquire firstly a sense of humour, and secondly the realisation that his actions encapsulate everything that is admirable about this country, everything that makes it unique in the world and worth defending, even in the face of a sustained attack by a political class who despise their own people and have betrayed their own heritage.

February 2003

GLITTERING PRIZE?

Rome, 800 AD, and Charlemagne, warrior leader, is in town. Accompanied by his Frankish knights, armed to the teeth, he tours the city, receiving adulation from the populace. That evening, by special invite from His Holiness Pope Leo III, Charlemagne attended mass in the Vatican church.

During the service, in full view of the congregation, the Pope produced a golden crown and placed it on the head of the unsuspecting Charlemagne, with more or less these words: "I hereby pronounce you Holy Roman Emperor."

This did not go down well. Charlemagne put a brave face on it, but said later: "Had I known what was planned, I would never have entered that church". In effect, he had been brilliantly "Gotchya'd" by the Pope, who wanted to unite Europe against the Arabs in the east.

Charlemagne's empire, covering much of Northern and Central Europe, was an ephemeral affair, and soon collapsed after his death. Yet 1,200 years later there are parallels with the European Union.

Like the EU, the court was an itinerant one, travelling in the wake of the Emperor (the EU shuttles back and forth every few weeks between Brussels and Strasbourg, uprooting all the secretarial staff, all the files, all the ancillary support, all at vast expense, all just to placate the French).

Also like the EU, Charlemagne believed in a single currency, worth 240 denarii to the pound. The present euro is about as popular as a rattlesnake in a bran tub but whether Charlemagne's version was better regarded is anybody's guess.

You may think it unfair to rope in this historical figure and parade him around as a representative of the EU, and I take the point, but I'm afraid that it's none of my doing. Every year, in May, the German city of Aachen awards the prestigious "Charlemagne Prize" to the personality who has made an outstanding contribution to the European Union. Former recipients include disgraced ex-Chancellor Kohl, Sir Edward Heath (less said about him the better), and in 1999, Tony Blair himself, our beloved leader.

The 2002 prizewinner surpassed even these luminaries. After much deliberation the panel awarded the prize to…(roll of drums, fanfare of trumpets)… the euro itself. That's right: they awarded it to the single currency.

The acceptance speech was extremely moving. Wim Duisenberg, head of the Central Bank, could barely contain himself: "The euro is the symbol of the European Union, and a bold step conceived as part of a wider process of uniting Europe not only economically but also politically."

A question. If the euro is so wonderful that it deserves the Charlemagne Prize, why do the Germans call it the 'Teuero?' In German the word 'Teuer' means expensive.

March 2003

RISE & SLIDE OF THE EURO

The euro has regained its original market value, which is good for Euroland and good for us (things we sell them become cheaper and therefore more competitive, helping our export figures). Our importers might disagree of course, and it makes a pizza in Rome or an ouzo in Athens more expensive.

Supporters of the euro are very pleased at this recovery. "Look", they say, "Perhaps the euro had a dodgy start, but now it's a genuine rival to sterling or the dollar".

But there is a problem with this, and it's a big one. Due to scandals with Enron, World-Com, Anderson, Tyco etc, investors unloaded dollars and bought gold, Swiss francs, and euros. Last week (at the time of writing) the dollar and the euro even reached parity.

Michael Hughes, head of investment at Baring Asset Management in London, explained what was going on: "We're anti-dollar, not pro-euro." And this is a crucial difference.

Eric Lonergan, global economist for Cazenove, also in London, said: "It's a short-term trading position, not a long-term investment strategy."

The euro-lovers are trying to sell the moon in the market place, but British customers are staying away in droves. Michael Winner, film director and columnist, referring to Europe's divisions over Iraq, wrote on 2nd March: "I was in favour of monetary union. But the idea of having our taxes and interest rates dictated by those pompous, inept morons in France and Germany is utterly absurd."

A more heavyweight contribution came from Nobel-

Prize winning economist Milton Friedman, interviewed recently in the German magazine 'Capital': "I believe Euroland will break apart in five to fifteen years. The people speak different languages and have different cultures. Those who care about democracy must distance themselves from the euro."

An important point was then put to him: surely the US dollar was a single currency, and it seemed to work ok. How could that mean the euro was doomed?

"There's no comparison," replied Professor Freidman. "Americans speak English and are ready to move to where there are jobs. If there's suddenly a problem in Texas, say, money can pour into the state from Washington. In Euroland only a tiny sum comes from Brussels. When the national currencies ended, the competitive disadvantages of the euro were immediately visible in the unemployment figures. That is the Achilles heel of the euro. And it was apparent from the start".

May 2003

FISH FINGERED IN SCRABSTER

Last December, in the Scottish fishing-port of Scrabster, they were unloading the catch onto the harbourside: boxes of daisy-fresh fat haddock, 70 kilos at a time, some vessels carrying 1,700 boxes. There was cod, too, plenty of it, along with halibut the size of dinghies. The fishermen on the quay could only stare in silence, perhaps with envy, perhaps with sadness, perhaps with nostalgia, for these fish were not 'British' nor were they from the European Union, which amounts to the same thing. They were Icelandic, and they were marvellous and mature, caught from a well-managed fishery by fishermen who understand the sea and know not to take too much. British fishermen, hunting the same catch in EU waters further south, were coming home with half a box, not enough to cover the fuel.

In 1976 Britain owned two-thirds of Europe's fishing area, and our largest renewable resource was sea-fish. Today only 2% of that industry remains. How did this come about?

Well... it was like this. When we joined the Common Market in the 1970's, Prime Minister Edward Heath was so relieved to get in that he gave them our fishing grounds, without even demanding access to the Mediterranean for our own fleet. With friends like this, who needs enemies? In terms of Shakespearian criticism Mr Heath played the king as if someone had just played the ace.

Mr Heath (now Sir Edward) wasn't the only one to leave our fishermen looking like stunned mullet. Robin Cook, then Foreign Secretary, signalled just how much he valued our fisheries by surrendering the grounds around Rockall to the EU, (the reason he gave was because nobody lived there). The French now fish these waters, and have wiped virtually everything out.

The EU's fishing policy is a microcosm of why it fails in everything it touches. The quota system is a political trading pot, resulting in millions of tonnes of perfectly good fish being thrown back into the sea, left to float dying on the surface.

Recognising that cod-stocks were in decline, the EU then granted licences to fish for sand eels. Only one problem: the staple diet of cod is sand eels.

For Spain, Portugal and France, new waters have now opened up, and this is a massive yet virtually unknown scandal. Third-World countries have been bullied into letting the EU vessels rampage through their fishing grounds, where traditional coastal communities survive on local seafood. In Mauritania, West Africa, for example, it is estimated that one EU boat hoovers up in a week the equivalent of the total annual catch of every traditional fisherman in the country added together. And when the EU has raped those grounds and destroyed a traditional way of life, the fleet will move on elsewhere.

For Britain, at least, there is only one solution. We must take control of our fishing grounds and run them properly. But we cannot do that if we're in the European Union. We must bite the bullet and leave the EU. And if I sound angry at what is happening to our country, that is probably because I am.

May 2003

With many thanks to Ian Bookless
(Country Illustrated magazine)

AN ICE CREAM WAR

Ivan Hall's been at it again, writing to the papers, accusing me of employing the propaganda methods of Dr Goebbels. There will always be some who are so convinced of their own right, despite the overwhelming evidence, that they are beyond reach, and Mr Hall is probably one of them. But the Goebbels charge should be answered, if only because there are some surprising parallels.

For example: I understand that all 5-year olds in British schools are now given EU 'Citizenship' lessons, accompanied by 'Euroquest', a glossy package which informs the children that the EU is 'like a club'... 'the more people who join, the more we can sell to each other'. Euroquest even trumpets the joys of the single currency. Goebbels would have approved: "To you parents, I say: We don't need you. We have your children."

Other booklets sponsored by the EU and aimed at youngsters are "Let's Draw Europe Together" (the first chapter is 'Europe My Country'), and the classic "The Raspberry-Ice-Cream War", involving a bunch of kids who go back in time to a world still blighted by sovereign nations and border controls, to teach the inhabitants about the wonders of political integration. Another favourite is "Captain Euro", a superhero who goes up against the evil "D-Vider". I suspect that Mr Hall might enjoy this one.

Daniel Hannan, MEP, a Tory who sounds a good egg to me, has unearthed these, including the EU's latest: the cartoon exploits of a feisty MEP heroine whose speech-bubbles contain such brilliant one-liners as: "You can laugh... wait until you've seen my amendments to the Commission proposal!" or the equally enjoyable: "We'll be getting the Council's common position soon. Then things will hot up!"

This comic strip has been translated into 22 languages to be distributed across the EU as an 'educational aid', funded by the taxpayers of Europe to brainwash our children.

As Mr Hannan adds: "In a crowded field this publication must rank as unintentionally the funniest produced by Brussels. One particularly fine touch is that the Strasbourg hemicycle is always shown full of

MEPs. In reality the chamber rarely contains more than 30 of the 626 members… except when they must be present in order to qualify for their allowances. Then the place is positively heaving".

August 2003

To see for yourself, go to **www.captaineuro.com**

BLOCKWORK AND INTEGRITY

During the 1964 general election, Graham Danton, weatherman, journalist, radio presenter, and newspaper columnist, was extending his kitchen. It was a dark night, and very cold. Graham was laying blockwork outside, working by the light of a bare electric bulb - probably wishing he'd got a professional to do the job - when the prospective Tory candidate put his head around the door. Mr Michael Heseltine, sporting his blue rosette. Could they have a little chat about the election?

Graham put him off: "I am sorry to inform you, Mr Heseltine, that I will be voting Liberal - for Mr 'Bloggs'. I admire his policies, his beliefs, his integrity and his single-mindedness". To which Heseltine replied: "I am sorry to inform *you*, Mr Danton, that 'Mr Bloggs' went over to the Labour Party eleven months ago." Which all goes to show the murky waters of politics and how easy it is for loyalty to be betrayed.

British politicians must be held in check by the media, not by the people, who are too busy paying the mortgage and working the tread wheel. Graham Danton is one of those journalists who deserve our continual respect and gratitude for voicing the feelings of the unsung majority, writing with a slightly

incredulous air on the antics of the European Union
and on the general background of betrayal from our
rulers, and that we have allowed this to happen.

Mr Danton is not alone. To quote Peter Hitchens, in
the Mail on Sunday, 22 December, 2002: "Following
the prosecution of a man for being rude to a Muslim,
we have the Muslims who won compensation after
they were sacked for disrupting the two-minute
silence following September 11.... I cannot be
bothered to be outraged by this; we are governed by
people who despise us... Our human rights are
camouflage for an assault on human freedom; (and)
the Tories are an obstacle to correcting any of these
things. Let them split soon, so a new movement can
sweep New Labour's rabble from office".

Graham Danton (along with Peter Hitchens) is that
rare thing: an honest man, not afraid to stick his head
above the battlements, showing some belief, some
passion, and... yes... some anger, in a grey world
where conformity is becoming law and rocking the
boat is forbidden, unless one rocks it in a certain way.
It's called freedom, and it's getting rarer every day.

May 2003

ENGLAND, ENGLAND

It happened so quickly, and nobody - not even those
who had planned it - expected the fall to be so fast. In
2005 the then-Prime Minister, Tony Blair, signed the
European Constitution, committing Britain to the EU
with no exit-route. The way was then clear for a
proper "Europe of the Regions". In London, judging by
the historical record and from the testimony of those
present at the time, few realised the implications. With

Westminster now by-passed, the British people looked to Brussels for political guidance. Most historians now agree that this was the defining period. Resentment and dissatisfaction among the populace culminated in The Trafalgar Square riots of 2007, with the loss of twelve lives.

The relocation of the financial and insurance markets to Frankfurt, and a concurrent (and huge) drop in investment from the United States, followed by a widespread slump in property values, led to the announcement of the Government's infamous "Austerity Budget" of 2008, and further unrest on the streets, resulting in the 2009 "Civil Emergencies Act", rushed through by an alarmed judiciary in Brussels. This saw armed police on routine patrol in every high street in Britain, carrying immunity from prosecution whilst engaged on EUROPOL business.

Within three months the Oath of European Allegiance, sworn by members of the police and armed services, had replaced the traditional Oath of Allegiance to the Crown. The subsequent departure of the Royal Family to the Isle of Wight saw the collapse of the tourist-based economy overnight (though in reality the Monarch's exile was forced, as the recently-published Osborne House papers now make clear).

First to declare independence was Scotland, then Wales, with both announcing the opening of their self-styled "Free Embassies" in various capital cities around the world. Appeals to the European Union from the English Regional Council were immediately (and very publicly) rebuffed by the EU Commission in a terse statement from the steps of the Elysee Palace: "The very notion of England as a separate political entity is not only a misnomer, it is irrelevant in a modern European context. The world has moved on".

By 2011, after various attempts at rescue, the EU concluded that England had become a hopeless case, and further funding was effectively curtailed. The Greenwich Meridian was replaced by Paris Mean Time, and in a sub-clause to the Treaty of Verona the EU withdrew from the English the right to free movement within the Union. It was felt that the English carried with them "the taint of failure".

As the writer and commentator Julian Barnes noted in his seminal work "England, England": 'From Dowager to Down-and-Out... Old England had lost its history, and therefore – since memory is identity – had lost all sense of itself.'

July 2003

THE SORT OF SCUM THAT READS THE SUN

Trevor Kavanagh is Political Editor of The Sun newspaper. Late one evening in October 2000, he sat down for a few drinks with a 30-something official in the British Foreign Office, a civil servant responsible for key negotiations with Brussels.

Asked by Mr Kavanagh what would happen if Blair couldn't win a referendum on the euro, the official seemed unworried: "Our strategy now is to get us signed up to so much else – foreign policy, justice, you name it – so that in the end joining the euro won't seem like a big deal." He went on to say: "Nationality is an irrelevance. To be honest I feel far more comfortable with the kind of people I negotiate with than I do with 'the people'. EU mandarins share an outlook, an education, a European culture. We all have far more in common with each other than we do with our respective LOWER classes."

Mr Kavanagh asked him, "Do you mean the sort of people who read The Sun?"

"Exactly", said the official. "My sister goes out with that sort of scum from time to time. Very depressing. As for the euro there should never have been a promise to hold a referendum. I mean, consulting the public on an issue as important as this is barking."

When I read things like the above (which appeared in The Sun on 30/10/00) it becomes clear that the only solution is a root and branch reform of the Foreign Office. Throw open the doors. These particular Augean Stables will need the River Thames to sluice them clean.

July 2003

ICH BIN EIN PULLOVER

If the world could agree on using one single common language we would avoid misunderstandings such as when President Kennedy travelled to Communist-encircled Berlin in the early 1960's, and told the cheering crowds: "Ich bin ein Berliner".... or "I am a doughnut", (A 'Berliner' is a sweet pastry). Another example is when President Jimmy Carter visited Poland in 1977 and informed them: "I wish to learn your opinions and understand your desires for the future." His own interpreter translated this as: "I desire the Poles carnally".

In his book, Mother Tongue, Bill Bryson described a few drawbacks to showing Hollywood movies in Europe. In one blockbuster a traffic-cop tells a speeding motorist to "Pull over", but the Italian translator has the officer asking for a sweater; whilst in a film with Spanish subtitles a character asks if he can bring a date to the funeral, which is translated into a request to bring a fig along with him.

Even computers can't bridge this gap. The phrase "Out of sight, out of mind", translated out of English and then back again, comes up as "Blind insanity". Talking of which, the European Union spends £1.5 Million every day on 4,000 translators in Brussels and Strasbourg, with things getting far, far worse as the EU enlarges.

Or perhaps having a single common language isn't such a great idea, after all. Perhaps we're better off with some healthy confusion... When an American airline executive describes a crash into a hillside as "an involuntary conversion of a 727", or when a Texas hospital refers to death as "a negative patient-care outcome", you know that you're in trouble. The Pentagon describes even the humble toothpick as "a wooden interdental stimulator".

Perhaps the best option is for the nations to keep their own identities, each with their own customs and foibles, language and currency. Going abroad should be different, strange and exciting. In short, it should be foreign. How tediously boring if everywhere eventually becomes familiar.

July 2003

GRAHAM BOOTH AND A VERY GOOD FISH IMPRESSION

It had been a busy day in Westminster, and the media were jostling for position on Parliament Green. Chancellor Gordon Brown had just announced the failure of his economic tests for joining the Euro. Among those being interviewed on the Green that day was Graham Booth, MEP for the UK Independence Party.

The interview, on Radio 4's "PM" programme, began with a briskly self-assured question from the lady-interviewer: "And now I'm talking to Graham Booth from the UKIP... Mr Booth, surely you're not suggesting that it's in Britain's national interest to withdraw from the European Union, with all the benefits we get from it?"

Graham replied: "Yes, I am.... Would you mind telling me what the benefits are?", upon which the poor girl did a very good cod impression, mouth working soundlessly, even over the radio.

Graham finished her off: "Exactly...Nobody ever can."

One reply to Graham's question is that among other things the EU has brought us VAT (making most things 15% or so more expensive at the stroke of a pen), locked our farmers into becoming subsidy junkies rather than producing food that people want in the real world; distorted the domestic food market (20% of our milk has to be imported, by law); forced us to separate our rail operators from those who run the track; split up the Post Office into Royal Mail, Counters, and Parcel force; virtually destroyed our fishing industry; and undermined core industries such as coal, steel and shipbuilding, often to the benefit of subsidised European competition, itself illegal under the rules of the Single Market.

In coal, the boss of RGB Mining (the successor to British Coal) said in 1999: "If I had the same subsidies as the Germans I could afford to give the stuff away."

As for British Steel, they were ruined and asset-stripped when they sold out their rock-hard name to

Dutch-owned "Corus". With a wet-weekend name like that, they didn't stand a chance.

In air-travel Bob Ayling, former boss of British Airways, did his politically correct part when he changed the Union Jack logo on the tail-fin of BA planes – squandering the 'Unique Selling Point' of BA, and costing them £-millions as customers chose to fly with other airlines. (Mr Ayling probably didn't mind: he received a large bonus when he stepped down, and remains one of the Prime Minister's closest friends. Let's ignore the losses to the shareholders and the wave of job cuts that followed after his period at the helm.)

Perhaps the best (or worst) thing that we have learnt from our experiment with the EU is how our own politicians from all across the spectrum have lied to us until they are blue in the face.

August 2003

AN "EU-FUNDED LOBBY GROUP"

Dr Frank Oliver is the local Chairman of the European Movement, funded by EU cash (which means that every tax-payer in Britain is subsidising his organisation.) and his statements to the media are revealing. For example, he is a great fan of the euro and derides anyone who disagrees with him. He will be busy in the coming months, given that most of us do not want the Single Currency.

In the newspapers recently Dr Oliver scoffed at a claim that the National Health Service would be in jeopardy if we joined the euro. These rumours came from "fanatical Europhobes", serving up "nonsense" and "alarmist tosh". Let's ignore the insults; they're rather endearing in a way and there is comfort in the familiar.

But I should explain that Oliver is an academic doctor, not medical, and very proud that his own students, year after year, vote him "Most Boring Lecturer" on campus at Exeter University.

As for the euro and the NHS, the good Doctor might be interested in a report from The Times (5th May) where the European Central Bank warned Gordon Brown that free health care would have to be restricted to emergency services only, otherwise the cost would overwhelm European economies and lead to soaring inflation. This bombshell first appeared in the ECB's own monthly bulletin, saying that Britain's ageing population would make tax-funded health services and long-term care unaffordable in the future.

Here is part of The Times' report: "Tax rises to meet the extra demands would soon become politically unacceptable and the sums in question would be too large to borrow, the ECB said. The article, which is published under the ECB's authority rather than being just a working paper by researchers, recommends swift reforms with patients paying for more private operations".

Dr Oliver concluded with a warning that we must make a final decision on the euro (and on the new European Constitution) and here I agree with him totally. That decision should be: Thanks for asking, but no. Never. Ever.

August 2003

A TRIP ROUND THE BAY

A few weeks before the European elections in 2004, Mick Mahon, (skipper of the 29' stern trawler J-Anne) will pack up his nets, hose down the decks and set out from Newlyn harbour. But this will be no ordinary trip around the bay. Drake's drum will be banging. Mick's destination is Traitor's Gate, the Tower of London. En-route, Mick and the J-Anne will call at south-coast ports for interviews with journalists from around the world, representing TV, radio and the newspapers.

The Daily Mail enthusiastically reported the plan a few weeks ago, with the headline 'Irates of Penzance', and such swashbucklers as: "Mahon has little in common with that other great sailor, Sir Edward Heath... Indeed if you mention Heath's name you get the most violent, timber-shivering crepitation."

As the J-Anne enters the River Thames, bedecked with British flags and UK Independence Party emblems, she will be joined by a second trawler, this one from the east coast of Scotland, completing a similar journey. Heralded by a hooting flotilla of Thames boatmen, Mick and his Scottish companion-vessel will moor outside Traitor's Gate, and - in the full glare of the world's media - then deliver copies of the various EU treaties signed by our spineless politicians over the last few years.

Mick is a fervent campaigner against the insane madness of the Common Fisheries Policy and the huge damage it has wreaked upon our once-great fishing industry. Even worse for Tony Blair, he's no stranger to the camera. The J-Anne has appeared on Weekend World, Panorama, Newsnight etc. But this time it will be different. This time the world will be watching.

July 2003

Mick Mahon did sail up the Thames, with plenty of coverage from overseas film crews. The UK media had other fish to fry.

AT THE HEART OF EUROPE

Take two European countries not in the EU... First, Norway (which has grown twice as fast as Britain over the last thirty years), and the words of Aslaug Haga, leader of the Centre Party: "Norway, we were told, would go down the drain if we didn't become members. That just didn't happen, did it? The fact that we're not in the EU didn't damage our economy at all – quite the opposite. Our unemployment is half the EU average. Nor have we ended up in total isolation, as the Yes campaign said we would. In fact, being outside the EU has actually been a help in terms of our international relations. We've been involved in the peace process in the Middle East and Sri Lanka in a way we would never have done if we'd been inside the EU."

Mr Haga went on: "I can't see any disadvantage in remaining outside. Of course, the prime minister and the foreign minister would like to eat cherries with the big boys and girls in Brussels, but that's how the political elite always think. Isn't it?"

Apart from her reserves of oil and gas, Norway also has massive stocks of fish in her 200-mile-wide territorial waters: "If the EU had had control of our fishing zone," said Orjan Olsvik, chairman of a firm with huge fishing interests, "these stocks would already have been destroyed. The Spanish armada would have taken everything."

And finally Switzerland, richest country in Europe... In 2002 the so-called 'Euroturbos' launched a campaign for entry into the Brussels club, but were struck dumb when 75% of Swiss turned them down in a referendum: "We were completely wiped out," admitted Professor Peter Tschopp, professor of economics at Geneva University. "We don't dare say anything more". And Jean-Jaques Roth, chief editor of Le Temps, recently said: "It's now political suicide to mention the EU. No-one would dare take the issue out of the box".

"The whole thing's getting too big", said Theo Phyll, a mountain farmer in central Switzerland. "It was like that in Russia. They became too big and then collapsed. I think it'll be the same with the EU."

When asked how the Swiss would have reacted if Tony Blair had denied them a vote on the EU Constitution, Farmer Phyll's response was blunt: "It could not possibly happen in this county. If it did, the people would demonstrate en-masse and the prime minister would be fired. Poodle (Blair's nickname in Switzerland) would simply have to go".

August 2002

A CLUNKING RIGHT AND LEFT

It's not just the so-called "Right-wing" who have set their faces against the euro. Now, the so-called "Left-wing" are making their voices heard, and not before time. Labour stars Harry Enfield and Rick Mayall have taken the lead in an apparently "spectacular" £1 million video, urging fans not to ditch the Pound, backed up by musician Jools Holland and comedians John Sessions and Phil Cornwell, along with Labour MPs Diane Abbot and former Government Minister Kate Hooey. Other stars are rumoured to be lining up in the wings. The video will appear alongside a blockbuster movie (possibly Spiderman) in cinemas around the country.

But for Tony Blair things have just got worse. Unison, Britain's biggest trade union, has just come out firmly against the euro, sending a leaflet to all its branches. The General Secretary, Dave Prentis, complained about the effect the euro would have on Gordon Brown's plans to increase public spending. He said: "We are not anti-Europe, but anti the single currency on its current terms. And we think that the Chancellor should adopt a sixth economic test which looks at the impact on our public spending".

A few weeks earlier, Brian Burkitt, a lecturer at Bradford University, wrote a devastating attack on the failures of the euro, which appeared not in the Telegraph but in the Left-Wing "Tribune". Dr Burkitt pleaded with his audience, "We need a restatement of the fundamental reasons why euro-realism (his words, not mine) is a left-wing cause, rather than a nationalistic right-wing one".

It gets even worse for the Prime Minister. A new ICM poll has just found that 41% of voters would prefer to keep the pound and have Gordon Brown in the top seat. Only 35% wanted Blair and the euro.

And just when it couldn't get any worse, Goldman Sachs, respected city investment bankers, estimated that joining the euro would add 3p to income tax and lead to cuts in the NHS and other public services of about £15 billion. No wonder Unison is so worried.

The final icing on the cake, and it was delivered with a flourish, came from the new President of the CBI, Sir John Egan, who gave it to the Government straight between the eyes: ""If your sole reason for going into the euro is that it will be better for business, then don't do it".

September 2003

WHERE TO STUFF THIS?

As I type this, I have in front of me a box-file stuffed with interesting snippets of information, but what to do with it all? Here's one now, a cutting from the Sun: "Euro Dead in Five Years: Prof"...The 'prof' - and he's not a happy man - is Carl Schactschneider, who predicts that the euro doesn't have long: "There will be a return to single currencies, but the mark won't come back because the trust in it is ruined. We sacrificed advantages for a European idea which was an illusion".

Or another clipping from the box: Daily Telegraph back in November: "Widow, 93, Wins Fight for Female Helper". Una Penny, 93, faced the loss of her home-help because she refused to be bathed by a male helper. South Gloucestershire Council told her family that she would have to be "psychiatrically-reassessed" to find out if she had problems with men. Her refusal to accept a male carer "would infringe his rights under the European Charter". The only reply to this is either a sad shake of the head or an armed uprising, just to clear the air.

On the subject of conflict, here is another one: "A Medieval Tradition", (the Guardian). During the One-Hundred-Years-War between France and England, our archers were a fearsome weapon against the mounted French knights. If the French captured an archer, they cut off the man's "two fingers" to prevent him using his longbow; hence the V-sign, used by our men at Agincourt in 1415 to inform the French that they were still very much in the game, thank you very much. When John Prescott, entering No 10, gave the press a two-fingered salute behind his back, one is tempted to ask if he was aware of that tradition. Knowing Prescott, this seems unlikely.

And just in case you feel that this is biased against New Labour, may I leave you with a final cutting, from The Times, 19 November, taken from the Conservative Group for Europe magazine, a guide to supporters of Kenneth Clarke who want ordinary Conservative members to adopt them as a candidate for the EU elections: "In current times it is important to be virulently euro-sceptic in your rhetoric and if this means concealing your real beliefs – don't worry. Remember two things: you are a politician, so lying comes naturally, and secondly it is just for one night. Tomorrow they will have forgotten your name, so you can go on being a federalist with a clear conscience".

My box of press cuttings and snippets grows by the day, but... just as with the above... I still haven't the faintest idea what to do with it all.

September 2003

JAMMY DODGERS

Austrian cake-makers have been diddling customers in Vienna and Salzburg by cutting back on how much filling goes into their buns and éclairs. But fear not. The ever-watchful guardians of the European Union are now on the case, warning that unless they change their ways the guilty bakers will face up to three months in jail... Quite right too: these Austrian Jammy Dodgers are a menace to society and should be taken into custody.

But should the same law apply here in Britain? Well, it soon could do, with an EU-wide justice system called Corpus Juris, literally "The Body of the Law", based on the old Napoleonic system, which will overrule our own.

In some cases it already does; try buying a pound of bananas in Sunderland and the local council will soon be crawling all over the stallholder who sold them to you, though strangely you can still buy a "Quarter-pounder" in McDonalds. One law for the big. Another for the small.... The more things change, the more they stay the same.

"Corpus Juris" will be enforced by Europol, the EU's own police force, currently being organised on the quiet. Under the new system a Europol officer would have the power to arrest you in Britain, without a warrant, without even giving a reason, and take you to any EU destination, where you could be held indefinitely, without either a court appearance, trial by jury, or even the presumption of innocence.

On the Continent it's usually up to the accused to prove their innocence. In Britain it's the State's job to prove that you're guilty. But signing up to the EU Constitution will throw away that independence.

One final point: Article 12, Chapter 5, of the Protocol on the Privileges and Immunities of the EU, makes it quite clear that Europol officers can invent it as they go along. "All officials and other servants... (of Europol)... should be immune from prosecution in respect of acts performed by them in their official capacity, including their words (spoken or written)...;

and also that they continue to enjoy immunity from prosecution even when they have ceased to hold office."

The document goes on to state that all premises and (EU) government buildings should be exempt from search, confiscation, requisition, or inspection. In other words this is a Get Out of Jail Free card for

Europol officers. As long as you are on EU-state business, no court can touch you. As for the accused, no member-state can stand up for them. Which perhaps explains why our own government, in the case of the Athens "Plane Spotters" affair, didn't order the Greek Government to drop the charges and release our people at once. This is the State of things to come, and - like most Austrian patisserie – it is no mere trifle.

September 2003

DEER-HUNTING AT AGINCOURT

The Iraq war has shown the naïve madness of having a common defence policy with the EU. The French and the Germans pretended to take the moral high ground but forgot to mention that Saddam owed them billions of euros for past shipments of military hardware. An allied invasion would wipe out that debt, and France, Germany and Russia would see their investment go up in smoke. Hence their opposition to toppling Saddam, and their scramble for US contracts once he'd gone.

Norman Schwartzkopf did not miss the great European Army, saying: "Going to war without the French is like going deer-hunting without your accordion", though I prefer David Letterman's wry comment: "The last time the French asked for more proof, it came marching into Paris under a German flag."

Regardless of one's own opinion on Iraq, the fact is that under a common defence policy the British people would have even less say than they do now (if that's possible).

We had another contretemps with the French, but this was 600 years ago on St Crispin's Day in 1415 at a place called Agincourt, where the English bowmen slaughtered 10,000 mounted French knights, the cream of the French nobility. As I have mentioned before, this was the origin of the V-sign, the English archers informing the enemy that they still had their bow-fingers, thank you very much.

There is another event planned for the same date (25th October 2003), though hopefully a less bloody affair than Agincourt. The UK Independence Party will be holding a Euro Election Launch Rally at The Great Hall, Exeter University, 10.00am-5.00pm, free admission and anyone is welcome. Food is available, but most importantly there is a bar. Among the speakers are Roger Knapman, UKIP leader and Dick Morris, who masterminded Bill Clinton's presidential campaigns. Should be an eye-opening day. Please try to get there if you can.

October 2003

COD IS DEAD

There is a smell of fish in the air... Thanks to the European Union our once thriving fishing industry is on its knees. British fishermen were sacrificed for a dim-witted dream of a united Europe. To those in power they were an embarrassing nuisance. Viewed as part of the problem, they were "politically insignificant" and have spent the last thirty years being stuffed down the EU-bend by successive Tory and Labour governments.

The crew of the "Ben Loyal", a fishing vessel out of Newlyn, recently produced a video called "Is This

Conservation?" in which the skipper, John Turtle and his crew, filmed themselves throwing back tons of perfectly good cod into the sea because they were over their quota. The quota system is the EU's lame-brained scheme to protect fish stocks, presided over by Fisheries Commissioner Franz Fischler, an Austrian who – surname aside – seems to have few qualifications for the job. (Austria is entirely landlocked).

Thousands of fish are dumped overboard every day by the European fleets, causing an environmental disaster as they sink to the bottom, to lie in a putrid decaying carpet across the seabed. Skipper Turtle says in the film: "While the British public are encouraged to believe how the European quota system is a successful conservation tool, nothing can be further from the truth. Few see the massive amounts of fish dumped each year to fall in line with EU quota limits – rules set by non-fishermen. It's crazy".

The solution is simple. We must withdraw totally from the EU and run our own fishing grounds again, for the benefit of Britain and British fishermen. Yet how ironic... Given the destruction of so many UK boats, we now have a perfect opportunity to allow the industry a breathing space. Foreign vessels could be excluded for a number of years, allowing fish-stocks to recover. One huge problem: this remedy will be ignored because it's against the Single Market. Titter ye not...we're not even allowed to organise a "Buy British" campaign because it's illegal under EU law. That's how low we've sunk.

October 2003

HOLIDAY SNAPS

It's only a snapshot, but I'd like to offer a reason why the European Union can never work. This comes from Brian Sewell's book "South From Ephesus", an autobiographical journey through the ancient sites of Turkey. In fairness to Mr Sewell I have no idea of his opinion on the European Union.

"The road to the Turkish border is littered with dead dogs. The dead dog sums up the difference between the Greek and the Turk. The Greek driver seeing a dog in the road a hundred yards ahead will accelerate and do his damnedest to run it down for sport; a Turk will maintain his speed and course, and if the dog happens to be in the way, will run over it – the one is vile, the other fatalistic, though I do not care for the indifference. I once scooped a kitten from the path of an Istanbul taxi with the speed and dexterity that I thought had left me when I stopped playing rugby – as the taxi shrieked to a halt the driver's scowl changed to laughter, but in Greece both I and the kitten would have been flattened".

There's bound to be some generalisation here (not all Englishmen have bowler hats; not all Frenchmen are gifted on the accordion) but contrast this with the response of most British motorists to, say, a family of ducks waddling down the road: there'd soon be a two-mile tailback, with nobody prepared to accelerate past.

It's only a snapshot, and perhaps a family of ducks means very little, but this is about how all of us - regardless of political viewpoint - would hopefully react in that situation. It is not a criticism of Greeks or Turks, merely recognition of the historical and cultural differences between us. If all three countries have such hugely different views about animals on the road, what chance with a common defence or immigration policy?

October 2003

HELLO EURO... GOODBYE NHS.

I'd like to quote from an article in the British Medical Association Journal (July 2003) by Sir Bill Morris, General Secretary of the Transport & General Workers Union. His words speak volumes.

"For those who still cling to the belief that early entry into the euro will not damage the NHS, I would recommend April's edition of the European Central Bank's Monthly Bulletin, which makes eye-opening reading.... Joining the euro comes at a sky-high cost: namely the retreat from universal health provision and the reining back of state investment in favour of the unfettered advance of the free market... For tax-payers now picking up the bill for NHS reform this report is the harbinger of doom – because the NHS they fund today may not be there tomorrow".

Sir Bill Morris is a bright man – simpletons do not run a Union like the TGWU and stay long in the job – and when a fully-paid up member of the Labour Party voices such concerns then it's time for even Guardian readers to wake up.

Sir Bill Morris continues on the ECB's report: "It exposes a motivating force driving the government's foundation hospital reforms. Having carefully studied the ECB report, I am persuaded that foundation hospitals are being introduced as a preparatory exercise for UK euro entry" (my italics).

He goes on: "The choice is simple: you can keep the NHS or you can choose a headlong rush into the euro. You cannot have both."

In fairness to Sir Bill (and to forestall criticism from the Blairite clones presently running our poor benighted country) he does add: "I still believe that the heart of Europe is the place where Britain should be and that the euro may one day be right for this country".

But may I suggest that there is a fundamental flaw in this thinking, echoing the Tory slogan "In Europe, not run by Europe"? As somebody once observed: "In the bear, not eaten by the bear". You're either in, or you're out. And if you are in, then you sign up to the rules. That's how it goes in a club. That's why it's time to get out, before this bunch of slimy chancers in Brussels totally wreck what's left of Britain.

October 2003

PART OF THE UNION

The game plan of the European Union is to make nationality an irrelevance. Loyalty will be owed to Brussels, of course, but loyalties such as British nationhood will be outdated. I neither hate nor fear Europe but I am not an 'EU-Citizen' and never will be.

In Britain this involves isolating England from the rest of the Union. The process is well underway. and it's called Regionalisation. Scotland has its Parliament, and Wales its Assembly. Northern Ireland is proving a problem for the forward thinkers in Brussels but they are assuredly working on it. As for England, we are being split up into eight 'regions', with London forming the ninth. This is a scaled down version of death by a thousand cuts, owing much to the Roman strategy of divide and rule.

To those who cry: "Regionalisation has nothing to do with the EU", may I point out that its full title is 'The European Union of the Cities and the Regions', and that the Maastrict Treaty allowing it to happen was signed by John Major.

The very survival of the UK is at stake. Parties such as Plaid Cwmri in Wales or the SNP in Scotland demand 'full independence from England', but all are committed to membership of the European Union. Any so-called independence would be a sham and a disaster. Left to the tender mercies of the EU they would be sidelined and overlooked, unable to make any real decisions, unable to make their voices heard among the polyglot cacophony of the EU debating chamber... leading them inevitably to the view that their former Union with England had been a golden time.

Other parts of the U.K have felt marginalized by London governments who may have come across as arrogant or indifferent at times... there have been lessons learnt on both sides, but I truly believe that Devolution has shown the huge danger of destroying the unity of the Union, a unity that has been painstakingly built up over the centuries, and one that we will squander at our peril.

October 2003

DOME-HEADED

When Tony Blair was trying to find exhibits to fill the Millennium Dome he was approached by a firm called Multimap, who had photographed the whole of Britain from the air, the result of which is available on the internet and on posters in every high street.

Multimap offered permission for the Prime Minister to incorporate the whole of Great Britain as a picture on the floor of the Dome. To most people this would seem a marvellous idea, a wonderful celebration of their country, offering visitors the chance to walk across their own town simply by placing their foot on the floor. But Tony Blair (or Bliar as some now refer to him) refused Multimap's offer, turning them down flat, saying: "It might offend people not born in Britain".... The logic defeats me, too.

Our wonderful Prime Minister is not alone in this bizarre attitude. Labour councillors recently tried to ban flying the St George's flag (on the grounds that it was offensive), whilst the Runnymede Trust announced that: "The word British is potentially racist", and our once-great BBC ordered its presenters not to wear Remembrance Day poppies because it might be "Confusing for foreign visitors".

If you ever work out what's going on, please let me know.

November 2003

THE TOWNIE PARTY

Simon Hart is the leader of the Countryside Alliance. Early last year a Labour MP took him to one side and told him: "The countryside represents everything that we despise – wealth, exclusiveness, feudalism, and cruelty – and we don't really care if that offends you".... Which doesn't leave much common ground between people like me who love the countryside, and senior figures in the Labour Party who clearly despise it.

The ban on fox hunting, the closure of village shops and post offices, the wilful near-destruction of our livestock farming, and the general collapse of British agriculture, (40% of farms coming onto the housing market are now bought by incomers, most of whom are fleeing the crime and filth of Labour's failed cities)... All this proves Tony Blair's innate hostility to the countryside. His plans to grow GM crops in Britain will be another nail in the coffin. More than 80% of the British people are opposed to GM, but if Blair gets his way, GM will be planted and our organic sector will be left to swing in the wind.

This arrogance is part of Mr Blair's make-up. The proposed EU Constitution is another example. Despite the fact that almost every UK political party now demands a referendum on the Constitution, the Prime Minister stubbornly refuses.

But there is a solution to this, and it's a good one. A postcard petition has been organised, addressed directly to Her Majesty the Queen, requesting her to withhold Royal Assent from this bill. More than 100,000 postcards have already been delivered to Her Majesty, but more need to be sent. The Queen's Chief Personal Secretary, Sir Robin Janvrin, has confirmed that: "The Queen has asked to be personally briefed on the number of postcards being received".... This is vitally important, and I ask you to order your postcards from "CREC",

66 Chippingfield, Harlow, Essex, CM17 0DJ. ...

Tel: 01279-635789. Alternatively, try their website: www.european-referendum.org.uk

If we don't fight now, our country will disappear before our eyes like conjurors' smoke... leaving Tony Blair and his zealots in control.

December 2003

2004

THETFORD, IN THE GOOD OLD DAYS WHEN EVERYBODY WORE A HAT

I have an old photograph...a print, to be exact. Sepia-tinted, margins fading into yellowy whiteness: this is the village street of Thetford in 1868. The street, shaded by a large tree, is empty. One grocer's shop, a blacksmith's, and a stationary cart... but no people. Not a soul. The place is deserted.

Except that it isn't deserted. Several people – farm-workers, ladies in bonnets entering the grocer's; a man on a horse perhaps; a few village dogs or the Blacksmith's cat - passed through this scene while it was being recorded. But they are invisible, all of them. The exposure of the photograph took sixty minutes; long enough for everyone to pass through without leaving a trace of themselves behind.

The author Penelope Lively noticed this, and posed the fascinating question: What would have happened if, half-an-hour into the exposure, someone had moved the cart or cut down the tree?

It is so easy to believe that we as individuals can never make a difference, that whatever happens will happen regardless. This suits those in power, who love a quiet time and a quiet electorate... One example is Tony Blair and his refusal to hold a referendum on the proposed European Constitution, which is of such vital importance that, like the euro, he cannot afford to ask us, the people, before signing away our country.

There is something that you can do, at the cost of a postage stamp. Please complete the petition below and return to The Office of Graham Booth MEP, Trago Mills, Newton Abbot, Devon, TQ12 6JD.

"A PETITION TO

THE RT. HON TONY BLAIR,

10 DOWNING STREET,

LONDON....

I, the undersigned, call for a national referendum on whether Britain should accept the new European Constitution or, alternatively, should replace EU membership with a single free trade agreement"

Name.........................

Tel no........................

Address.....................

[As a result of this petition hundreds of forms were received at Graham Booth's office and presented to the Prime Minister... a small part of the wider (and thankfully successful) campaign to force him into a change of mind]

January 2004

OUT FOR A QUICK SPIN

Ahead of us on the motorway is the mouth of a tunnel, signposted: "United States of Europe". The Lib-Dems are in a Porsche in the fast lane, flat out at top speed. They can't **wait** to get there.

In the middle lane, at a commendable 70mph, New Labour have chosen a people-carrier. Tony Blair is driving, but Gordon Brown - having studied the roadmap – is now reaching the horrible conclusion that maybe they went wrong a few miles back.

In the slow lane the Conservatives are in an old pick-up, overloaded with baggage, smoke belching from the exhaust; no tax or MOT, with front wings made of filler, dodgy brakes and no insurance. Someone has written 'KLEEN ME!' on the tailgate. The occupants are fighting over the wheel. This is an accident waiting to happen.

But there is another lane that the other three have overlooked, and it is occupied by the UK Independence Party, leading to a slip-road off the motorway, an escape route from the approaching smash called the European Union. As voters you have a choice to make. Which of these four, the only four that really matter; will you climb aboard? All roads do not lead to Brussels.

January 2004

LEFT-HANDED PAINT

The British still have a good sense of humour. In the workplace, staff-members are sent off for left-handed screwdrivers, striped paint, sky-hooks (my personal favourite) and the long weight (20 minutes is usually long enough), or a request for blue sparks for the grinder: "I'm out of blue ones, lad. Go back and ask 'em if red'll do." Or in the military: "If you're smiling, you don't know what's going on", and the old classic: "The Germans fire, and the British duck. The British fire, and the Germans duck. But when the Americans fire, everybody ducks".

Or in the Diplomatic Service, when various embassy officials were asked what they most desired for Christmas: the French ambassador wished for world peace, the Brazilian ambassador wanted an end to Third World poverty, and the British ambassador said he was hoping for a bottle of whisky and a box of chocolates.

This is all very well, but even a great sense of humour can wear thin. The damage inflicted on Britain by our membership of the European Union is enough to wipe the smile from anyone's face, and the UK Independence Party is now doing its best to tell the British People what has happened, what has been done in their name by those whom they trusted.... At times it seems a struggle, but as Nigel Farage MEP said recently: "Water finds its own level. So does political will. A small political party telling the truth will triumph over a larger one telling a lie."

May I finish with something from Dick Morris, American political guru and former campaign manager for Bill Clinton: "How do you spell NO to the EU, in English?

The answer is easy: U...K...I...P..."

January 2004

UNDER THE HAMMER

Farmer Joe Thompson took his wife to Carlisle market in 1832 and put her up for auction. "Gentlemen," he addressed the crowd, "I have to offer my wife, Mary Anne Thompson, to sell to the highest bidder. She has been to me only a born serpent...my domestic curse, a night invasion and a daily devil. May God deliver us from troublesome wives. Avoid them as you would a roaring lion, a loaded pistol, cholera, Mt Etna, or any other pestilential thing in nature".

Mr Thompson listed his wife's good points: "She can read novels and milk cows; she can laugh and weep with the same ease that you could take a glass of ale. She can make butter and scold the maid; she cannot make rum, gin, or whisky, but is a good judge of their quality from long experience in tasting them. I therefore offer her, with all her imperfections, for the sum of fifty shillings".

Mary Thompson was knocked down for twenty shillings, with a Newfoundland dog thrown in. The practise of men selling their wives, medieval in origin, was still fairly common in those days – it was cheaper and quicker than a divorce – and I propose the reintroduction of this practise, though not with the selling of wives but with our membership of the European Union...

"Ladies and Gentlemen, I offer you our membership of the Federal States of Europe... the disadvantages are manifest, huge, and cripplingly expensive; the advantages slight, fleeting and transient. I commend to you the huge raft of over regulation, the interference with domestic affairs, the sleaze and corruption of bloated and unaccountable bureaucracy, bereft of all control and driven by its own self-important self-advancement; the lack of democratic accountability; the loss of influence on the world stage... all of these - and much, much more - I heartily recommend to you.

Who will bid £25 billion, the latest estimated total annual cost of our membership? Then who will at least make an offer? Ladies and Gentlemen, surely at least an offer?"

January 2004

THE ICARUS SYNDROME

Printed on the bottom of a tub of Tesco's tiramsu: "Do not turn upside down". Or on a frozen dinner: "Serving suggestion: defrost". Or on a Stihl chainsaw: "Do not attempt to stop chain with hands." They obviously think we're not too tightly wrapped, one sandwich short of a picnic, (though after hearing about the man who burnt himself when ironing a shirt he happened to be wearing at the time, they might have a point).

If we're buried in useless information (e.g.: on a packet of Sainsbury's nuts: warning, contains nuts) then we probably won't notice the vitally important nuggets that really do matter. Which is a lengthy way of saying that Tony Blair will not be holding a referendum on the euro, despite all the gossip and speculation. Instead, he plans to bring it in by the back door.

It will work like this. The European Union is presently drawing up a constitution for itself, but it needs to be ratified by the British Government in 2004. The Foreign Office has confirmed there will NOT be a referendum on this, despite the fact that it will hand huge areas of national interest to the EU, giving the people "dual citizenship" and elevating the EU into a "single legal personality". Crime, asylum, and immigration will be handed to Brussels.

On 8 November, 2002, Tony Blair made a speech in Cardiff and revealed all: "We want more Europe, not less"... He is planning to give away most of the functions of the Foreign Office, Home Office, Lord Chancellor, and the MOD, all without a referendum; and once those have gone, the way to the euro is easy.

By then Labour will have fought the 2005 election, Gordon Brown can be safely sacked if he gives trouble, and under the EU constitution (binding all signatories to an oath of allegiance and to "refrain from any action contrary to the Union or likely to impair its effectiveness") Brussels can impose the euro on an unwilling Britain.

Some will scoff at this: "Utter loony nonsense. Paranoid drivel!"... Perhaps. We'll see. But I'd like to leave Mr Blair with a final warning, this on a Superman outfit: CAUTION. WEARING THIS COSTUME DOES NOT ENABLE YOU TO FLY!

February 2004

A MATURE AND WELL-ROUNDED APPROACH

If a political opponent congratulates you on your "mature approach to the debate", that's when you know you've lost – as anyone campaigning against a by-pass or village school closure will testify. On Britain's withdrawal from the European Union I remain childish.

Take the euro: those who support it really don't care whether it is good for ordinary Britons. When the euro lost 25% of its value, the Jeremiahs warned that UK exports to Europe would suffer. But after 9/11 when many US investors bought euros, pushing its value to an all-time high, we were then told that the weak dollar made it 'vital' for Britain to join the euro. As an intellectual argument this is emptier than a hermit's address book. The message seems to be: whatever the euro does, we should join it.

On a lighter note even Gordon Brown's own constituents are opposed to ditching the Pound. At the Partners bar in Cowdenbeath, landlord Andrew Kirk conducted a straw poll among his customers. Eleven voted against the euro; one voted in favour. But when quizzed it turned out that he'd thought he was being offered another drink, and was equally against the single currency.

As customer John Sharp, a mechanical engineer explained: "How many penny caramels could you get for £1 before decimalisation? You could get 240. The next day you could get 100. That's a con"... Or taxi driver Tom Louden: "You can tell them to stuff their euro. It's like when we went decimal, every price went up."

If, to euromaniacs, this seems an "immature approach", do you know something? Frankly I couldn't give a gobstopper.

February 2004

WINNING THE BATTLE BUT NOT THE WAR

The infamous "EU Constitution" has passed from the headlines. But it will return, in a different form. So let's look at some of those who tried to peddle it to us. Labour M.P. Keith Vaz, former Europe Minister, claimed it had "less significance than the Beano". Well, huge sections of the British Press clearly disagreed in 2003: The Times Opinion column (10th Feb) "Allez, Giscard! Europe is not a home for slaves", or the Daily Mail, (May 8th) "A blueprint for tyranny", or The Sun (12th Dec) "NO SURRENDER! We go into action as Blair prepares for sell-out to EU."

Peter Hain (another former Europe Minister) famously called it a "tidying up exercise", adding that three-million British jobs depended on EU membership. He reached this figure by misquoting the findings from a think-tank, the director of which had already described such misinformation as "Pure Goebbels". Even Mr Hain wrote in 1995 that handing control of Britain's economy to unelected officials in Frankfurt would be: "economically disastrous and politically dangerous."

Less well-known here is Jo Leinen, a German MEP, and Vice-chairman of the Committee for Constitutional Affairs in Brussels. In October 2002, he wrote: "Many people in Europe are still unaware of the important changes that are under way for the political structures in which they live. A referendum campaign would be the catalyst to create a public debate about these questions..."

But the sting follows one paragraph later: "The Constitution shall be deemed 'approved' if a majority of member states and a majority of EU citizens vote in favour of it. We have to move beyond an idea of Europe where a single member state can block the progress of all," (text highlighted by me).

In other words, if the rest of the EU votes "Yes" to the Constitution, with Britain saying "No", then Herr Leiden thinks it should be forced on us regardless. And they wonder why the UK Independence Party is campaigning for Britain's total withdrawal.

Most of us are loyal to this country, but it seems to me that Tony Blair has transferred his loyalty to Europe. In a speech to his Sedgefield constituency back in 1983, he stated: "The European Union is bad for Britain and bad for British jobs". Mr Blair has clearly moved from that position, but no man can serve two masters. Ultimately, inevitably, he will be forced to choose between them.

February 2004

PUB NAMES

Near Exeter is a pub called the Cat & Fiddle, named after Caton le Fidele, boyfriend of King Edward II in the 12th Century. In London the Elephant & Castle owes its name to the Infanta de Castile. Other pub names are more obvious: The Royal Oak or Golden Hind. There is longevity to these old names; they endure, and survive for a reason, capturing the mood of the time, outliving passing trends. So...if the euro-lovers win the day...which names might adorn our watering holes in a hundred year's time?

How about The Fisherman's Woe (the painted sign hanging outside has a redundant trawler broken up on the beach), The Rusty Plough (self-explanatory), The Foot In Mouth (a pile of burning cattle artfully depicted against the evening sky), and its variant The Shepherd's Warning.

Other possibilities are The Constitution Arms (a set of handcuffs), The Consort's Grimace (Cherie Blair smiling down, unlikely to be popular), or The Europol (no lock-ins, by order); and maybe the best of all: The Channel Funnel, depicted by a queue of 73-million citizens of former Soviet satellite and Balkan countries, each and every one of whom will have the right to move to Britain if Westminster ratifies the EU Constitution.

After that little lot, I think I need a drink.

March 2004

STAR GAZEY PIE

Last Christmas - for about three seconds - I almost felt sorry for fisheries minister Ben Bradshaw. But then it passed, and I felt better again. The Minister had spent Christmas week in Brussels, haggling over fish quotas, when he would have preferred to be in Exeter in his pinny, decorating the tree or whipping up a pudding.

At the end of the fishing negotiations Mr Bradshaw announced that he was pleased with the outcome: "The deal was criticised by some conservationists but moderate voices on both sides welcomed it".

In the Bradshaw universe, 'moderates' are those who agree with horse-traded deals, cooked up in Brussels between members of the EU who are helping themselves to our fish and driving stocks to extinction. Those who raise objections - the UK Independence Party, the World Wildlife Fund and the fishermen themselves - are not 'moderate'.

If this seems odd coming from a government minister, do remember that we are talking New Labour here, where spin reigns supreme, 'up' means 'down', and defeat becomes victory. As for Mr Bradshaw, to mangle the Duke of Wellington: "I don't know what the enemy will make of him, but he scares the hell out of me." This transient politician needs to be reminded that Britain has had enough of begging like performing seals for the return of our own fish.

The solution is for all our fishermen to smash up their boats on the beach, and find jobs on dry land. Then we won't need a Fisheries Minister. Problem solved. You will be pleased to know that this is already underway.

Alan Westlake and John Newton were fishermen in the East Devon village of Beer. They gave up their commercial fishing licences in July. Now they run trips around the bay for tourists. Mr Westlake said:

"We are among the last of Beer fishermen who carried on a family tradition, which in my case goes back at least four generations – so a way of life is now over among what is Beer's oldest fishing family."

Over the last 20 years the Beer fleet has dwindled from 14 boats to four. Dredging by foreign fleets in Lyme Bay has damaged the seabed, reducing shellfish catches. One of the surviving Beer fishermen, Kim Aplin, said: "There are only a few of us left, and we are sorry to see Alan and John go."

March 2004

A TRUE AND FAIR ACCOUNT

This may seem as dull as ditchwater, but please read on, if only because each of you is paying for it in many ways...

Every year the European Union presents its annual accounts – just like Trago Mills, ICI, or a jobbing plumber at the end of your street. If the taxman is not satisfied with what he sees, then the business is investigated, and more tax is demanded or a criminal investigation is launched.

But guess what. The EU is a law unto itself. Basic financial records, such as a fixed asset register, are not kept. There is no double-entry bookkeeping system, and 'Advances of funds to third parties' are treated as expenditure, which is fraudulent (they should be recorded as creating a debtor).

It gets worse: cash assets of the European Communities are 'unconfirmed' and bank accounts are unreconciled. No reconciliation of cash/bank balances means that no figures whatsoever produced by the EU can be relied upon in any respect.

Jens Peter-Bonde (a Danish MEP) and Jeffery Titford, (MEP for the UK Independence Party) called for an inquiry into this in 1999, which resulted in the mass resignation of the entire European Commission, including our own much-loved Neil Kinnock... But Mr Kinnock, who is nothing if not a survivor, was then reappointed and given the title of 'Anti Corruption Supremo' He, in turn, appointed a very bright Spanish accountant named Marta Andreasen to pinpoint waste and generally sort out the accounts.

Three months later, in early 2002, she made a damning report accusing the EU of failing to meet even basic accounting standards. The possibilities for fraud were virtually unimaginable. As a result she was sacked by Mr Kinnock, who also tried – unsuccessfully – to prevent her appearing before an EU parliamentary commission.

The EU Court of Auditors said in their report: "Failures abound", which perhaps explains why for the ninth year running the auditors have failed to approve the accounts. Any British businessperson pulling that stunt would find themselves behind bars before they could say "Porridge".

Unlike those who abuse the rules (such as 'Enron', the US Company, which collapsed in 2002, or Parmalat, the Italian food giant which recently went down like a led zeppelin), the EU's own very system of accounting is itself fraudulent. As described by Marta Andreasen – who should know better than anyone – the system can never comply with International Accepted Accounting Standards, or with the UK Generally Accepted Accounting Principles.

To quote Jeffery Titford: "The EU finances are a joke, but not a very funny one. The British Government is under an obligation to act in a responsible manner when spending public money. Handing billions of pounds of taxpayer's money every year to an organisation that does not even have double-entry bookkeeping makes an absolute mockery of that obligation."

March 2004

DIFFICULTIES OF EDUCATING PORK

You can never tell with a judge, but sometimes the jury can be far worse. Jerry Williams, from Little Rock, Arkansas, was awarded $14,500 after being bitten on the backside by his neighbour's beagle whilst it was chained up in its own yard. Mr William's award was less than sought because the jury felt that the dog might have been provoked by the fact that Mr Williams had climbed into the yard and repeatedly shot at it with an airgun.

Another example is Amber Carson of Lancaster, Pennsylvania, who won $113,500 damages from a restaurant after slipping on a soft drink and hurting her back. The beverage was on the floor because 30-seconds earlier Ms Carson had thrown it at her boyfriend during an argument.

My own favourite (though it may be an urban myth) is Merv Grazinski, of Oklahoma City, who purchased a brand-new 32-foot Winnebago motor home. On his first trip along the freeway, he set the cruise control to 70mph, and went through into the cabin to make himself a cup of coffee. The vehicle left the road and crashed.

Mr Grazinski sued Winnebago for not mentioning in the owner's manual that the vehicle did not drive itself... Incredibly the jury awarded him $1,750,000 and a new motor home.

Sometimes it works the other way, as in a recent British example: Brian Kent, a lorry driver, arrived in Dover from the cross-channel ferry with a consignment of Swiss wrapping paper. He had earlier alerted French Customs that his lorry had been interfered with, but they apparently found nothing.

When he reached Dover he noticed that the tilt ropes securing the rear doors had been tampered with, so he alerted British Customs. The vehicle was inspected and seven Iraqi and Iranian stowaways were discovered.

Mr Kent was immediately fined under the 1999 Asylum & Immigration Act, to the tune of £100,000. Quite understandably he refused to pay, and his lorry was confiscated, wrecking his livelihood. At the trial, Judge Peter Cowell said: "How did it come about that a decent Englishman of good character, responsible for finding stowaways, leading to their lawful detention, could be penalised in this way?... a more deserving case would be difficult to imagine".

As Mr Kent said: "I thought I was doing the right thing. But in hindsight I wish I had just kept quiet and let the refugees go"...

Sometimes the law is about as much use as a one-legged man in a backside-kicking contest.

March 2004

GUINNESS AND A SHRIMP CURRY

Murphy's Law states that if something **can** go wrong then it will go wrong, but Murphy had a friend called O'Toole, who always thought that Murphy was an optimist. Our membership of the European Union is a classic case of O'Toole's Variant... particularly something called "Gold-Plating", which works like this.

Brussels now makes most of our laws, rules and regulations, (current total, an incredible 200,000 and rising). But when those rules arrive here in London, the British Government often interprets them in a totally different way to how they were originally intended when first drawn up in Brussels... This is called "Gold-Plating", and not only is it totally self-inflicted, but it costs us a fortune.

For example, the Department of Trade & Industry's budget has increased by 44% in the last four years, mostly to create new layers of EU regulatory bureaucracy, usually by 'Statutory Instrument' which has no Parliamentary scrutiny. This army of pen pushers is paid by every taxpayer in Britain to enforce rules that (for the most part) are damaging to British interests.

A further problem is that our EU partners ignore Brussels directives at the drop of a hat, which makes the whole process about as useful as a chocolate poker: France has 544 cases outstanding, Italy 496, and Germany 440. In Britain, we implement - and often "gold-plate" - every single one of them. And when Poland joins the EU its 40 million population – most of whom subsist at poverty level in agriculture – are unlikely to rush to implement EU regulations on the length of a cow tether or the dimensions of a potato.

On the very day of writing this it was announced that

a further £37-billion is required when the EU enlarges, just to pay for the ten new entrants.... Gordon Brown calls this "Totally unacceptable", but the Lib-Dems have said: "We can't have Europe on the cheap. We must pay up". And as things stand they are dead right. "Europe" is not cheap, and Gold-Plating makes it even more costly.

I prefer Auric Goldfinger's advice to 007, as they sat down to a shrimp curry: "Mr Bond, the surest way to double your money, is to fold it and put it back in your pocket"... We could do with someone like Goldfinger around here at the moment.

March 2004

COUNTING MRS ARISTOTLE'S TEETH

'Thinking That You Know' is a trap we all fall into occasionally. Aristotle, the Greek philosopher, once wrote that women have two less teeth than men. He only needed to ask Mrs Aristotle to open her mouth and he would have discovered his error. But he didn't. And if Aristotle can do it, then so can anyone.

On Britain's membership of the European Union, there are still a few diehards who think that they know that it's a good idea - despite all the evidence to the contrary - and that's when a civilised discussion becomes difficult.

The writer Peter Hoeg captured this perfectly: "Very few people know how to listen. Their haste pulls them out of the conversation, or they try internally to improve the situation, or they're preparing what their next speech will be when you shut up and it's their turn on the stage."

A good example of this is Labour MEP Gary Titley. Before he became New Labour's leader in the Brussels Parliament, he said: "I am not a supporter of British membership of the single currency, and events since the launch of the euro have not persuaded me to change my mind."

But now, with his new job underway, he has released this statement: "For those who argue we can afford to delay, I say that for as long as we remain outside the euro, business in Britain will continue to fight for jobs and prosperity with one hand tied behind its back."

April 2004

HOW TO FIDDLE YOUR MEP EXPENSES

Giles Chichester, Tory MEP, is panicking. With the forthcoming European elections, he has been attacking the UK Independence Party's performance and attendance record in Brussels. So let's dig a little deeper into this.

Due to expansion of the European Union our country now faces the prospect of an unknown number of people emigrating here from the ten new member-states (total population 73-million), with who knows what consequences for education, transport, healthcare, and crime.

The Tories (who conned us into joining in the first place) voted "Yes" for EU expansion: only UKIP voted "No".... Mr Chichester can bluster as much as he likes, but I trust the British people to make the right choice at the European elections in June, and I predict that he will soon be joined by quite a few more MEP's from UKIP.

Let's look at a few wheezes carried out by MEPs, and this is jaw-dropping stuff for those who still believe in the "Euro-Ideal" ... Air travel: always reimbursed at business class, plus 20%. Wheeze: take Ryanair from Stanstead to Strasbourg (cost is £40 return, EU allowance £756...Pocket £716).

Or you can take the car, at 60p a mile. Wheeze: share the car from Brussels to Strasbourg with three MEPs, each of them claiming £170. A nice earner...

For holidays: £2,230 a year for working trips. Wheeze: get a friendly Greek or Spanish MEP to invite you for summer-time 'study of coastal tourist industry'.

Mr Chichester mentioned UKIP's attendance record at the EU. Setting aside the obvious point that three MEPs can't be everywhere at once, at least they cannot be accused of milking the system, unlike the other parties who religiously claim their £160 a day attendance expenses. Wheeze: sign on in Strasbourg on a Thursday and fly home, still getting paid for Friday when Parliament does not sit. Even better: sign on in the morning then spend the rest of the day playing golf. Or even better: stay at home and get someone else to fake your signature.

Generally this is not even about fraud. It is the whole rotten EU system. The only MEP who has ever been seriously pursued by the EU is Nigel Farage (UKIP) who was asked in 2001 to return £10,500 after he handed over unspent travel allowances to anti-EU causes including a London butcher who defied the ban on selling beef on the bone. "They said I was defrauding European taxpayers", Nigel said gleefully, "which I thought was delightfully upside-down".

April 2004

THANK YOU

Charlie Coburn was once a very popular actor and music hall entertainer. When asked the secret of his success, he explained: "I sang them my song and they didn't like it. So I sang it again, and they still didn't like it. So I sang it a third time, and one of them thought that he might get to like it if I changed the words and altered the music. So I sang it again – without changing a thing – and then they all liked it."

UKIP's success at the June 10th European Elections has rocked the entire political establishment to the core, because it was true People Power, in the face of media ridicule or indifference, with only a handful of wealthy supporters prepared to put their money where their beliefs were... Among them Bruce Robertson (Chairman of Trago Mills), Paul Sykes, and Alan Bown. And on behalf of UKIP I would like to thank them for their courage, patience, patriotism, and faith in the British people.

There are a few others to thank. All the MEP and local candidates (successful or not); the leadership who had the good sense to engage both Dick Morris (Bill Clinton's former advisor who told us to use billboards) and Max Clifford (who convinced Robert Kilroy-Silk to join us)

Also, Cornishman Mick Mahon, skipper of the J-Anne, who sailed his boat up the Thames in protest at the Common Fisheries fiasco. How interesting that when he called at Folkestone en-route he was told that the port was "Full" and he couldn't come in. Purely a coincidence that the owner of Folkestone harbour is a good friend of Mr Howard, the Tory leader. The words "political panic" spring to mind.

Others need to be thanked. During the Election

members and supporters of UKIP have erected signs and hoardings across the country; have tramped the streets, delivering leaflets, risking their fingertips every time they stuffed something through a letterbox only to have somebody's dog skidding towards them with a triumphant yelp down the hallway.

Finally, as regards the South-West office at Bovey Tracey, I'm sure that everyone in UKIP will join me in thanking Malcolm Wood, regional organiser, Sue Palfrey (of virtually infinite patience and calm, as I know from personal experience – she should take up plate-spinning as a hobby), Roger Bullock, and all of the volunteers who gave their time to man the 'phones, deal with enquiries, and do all that tedious stuffing of envelopes. When I first called into the office and saw the sky-high morale, I knew that something very special indeed was happening.

The final thanks go to the most important group – the British voters who recognised the truth when they saw it, and voted to save their country. To each and every one of you...THANK YOU very much indeed.

June 2004

With hindsight, Mr Kilroy-Silk was a double-edged sword. UKIP benefited, but cut its finger.

LOWERING THE BAR

This is all true... and comes from a book called 'Disorder in the American Courts', a record of cross-examinations compiled by long-suffering court reporters. The lawyer's questions are in ordinary typescript, and the replies from the witness (a medical doctor) are in italics:

Question... "Now doctor, isn't it true that when a person dies in his sleep, he doesn't know about it until the next morning?"...

Answer... *"Did you actually pass the bar exams?"*

Q... "Do you recall the time that you examined the body?"

A... *"8.30pm".*

Q... "And Mr Dennington was dead at the time?"

A... *"No, he was sitting on the table wondering why I was doing an autopsy"*

Q... "Before you performed the autopsy, did you check for a pulse?"

A... *"No".*

Q... "Did you check for blood pressure?"

A... *"No".*

Q... "Did you check for breathing?"

A... *"No".*

Q... "So, then it is possible that the patient was alive when you began the autopsy?"

A... *"No".*

Q... "How can you be so sure?"

A... *"Because his brain was sitting on my desk in a jar".*

Q... "But could the patient have still been alive, nevertheless?"

A... *"Yes, it is possible that he could have been alive and* *practising law somewhere".*

Not all lawyers are so ponderous. New Labour and the Conservatives are both led by ex-barristers, and Messrs Blair and Howard are equally slippery. On the EU Constitution, Tony Blair said that it was not essential for the UK to sign up. But when his ally (the Centre Right Spanish government) lost their recent general election after the Madrid bombings, he then told us that it was suddenly vital for Britain to join up without delay.

As for Mr Howard, although he opposes the EU Constitution, he refuses to scrap it (or offer a referendum) should the Conservatives win next time.... He has already stated that withdrawal from the EU is not an option

As UK Independence Party MEP Nigel Farage said: "Mr Howard is terrified of the split within the Conservative Party that a threat to leave the European Union would create. It's business as usual at Tory headquarters – putting party before country just as John Major did when he signed the Maastrict Treaty."

June 2004

PIECES OF EIGHT, PIECES OF EIGHT

A few weeks ago Glyn Ford MEP (Labour) accused me of parroting the BNP, and being "really just the same". He also attacked the UK Independence Party, but was about as convincing as Tony Blair on a good day. To quote the architect Sir Edwin Lutyens: "My answer to that is in the plural...and they bounce."

If I supported the BNP then I would belong to that organisation. The very fact that I don't – and also that UKIP has expelled a number of BNP infiltrators – should cause Mr Ford to pause for thought.

On my criticism of multiculturalism, I am totally unrepentant. If one day I sell up and move to France, I'll learn the language and immerse myself in French culture, hopefully without losing the part of me that is naturally "English"... But most importantly I will not expect France and the French to change their way of life, their modes of expression, nor their own French view of French history...

For me to relocate to France would be something of a return: my Challice ancestors were Huguenot silversmiths, who fled to England to escape religious persecution, so I am certainly not in favour of pulling up the drawbridge and declaring Britain a fortress. The tragedy is that political correctness has left this subject pretty much a no-go area, and Mr Ford provides a perfect example of why.

If one criticises unrestricted immigration (and the intellectually-bankrupt concept of multiculturalism) then with the predictability of one of Pavlov's dogs the Liberal Left screams "BNP" or "Racist", exactly the tactic that feeds support for the BNP. Mr Ford should be grateful to UKIP, but he probably isn't.

A few facts: 90% of asylum seekers are not fleeing persecution and fail the test of being a refugee. They are economic migrants and here illegally. Therefore they are illegal immigrants and should never have come to this country... With virtually open borders there is also the potential threat from terrorists, drug-dealers, and the East European Mafia. The British Government – for all its "War on Terror" – is so hamstrung by political correctness that it is failing the security of the British People.

We are one of the least "racist" or "extremist" countries in Europe. Think back to the 1930's when Fascism took hold in France, Germany, Spain, Rumania, Hungary, and Italy. Here in Britain Sir Oswald Mosley's Blackshirts were a mile away from achieving power.

On the whole it takes a lot to stir up the Brits, who generally like a quiet life, but the combination of political correctness and EU lies, might just have done the trick. This might also explain why New Labour are shipping in immigrants by the lorry load: 90% of them will become Labour voters in gratitude. Shameless gerrymandering.

Although I dislike playing Mr Ford's game, I should also point out that in the June elections the UK Independence Party fielded a number of candidates from "ethnic minority backgrounds" (not that that should matter one jot, but I suspect that Mr Ford might be interested) and those same UKIP members echo exactly the same words as myself: We need to control immigration, not shrug the issue away with patronising references to Tikka Masala being a sign of multiculturalism.

Finally, Anthony Brown, a Times journalist and son of an Indian immigrant, was told recently by a Middle Eastern friend (passionately pro-British) "This is not the country I came to in 1958. Britain is losing Britain in a fit of absent-mindedness. It is utter madness what is going on".

Another friend, this time from Nigeria, told him: "I can't believe that Britain is just letting herself go."

Well I'm afraid that I can... With our present Labour Government we are walking into a disaster of the greatest magnitude and anything is possible.

June 2004

I AM HOLDING THIS PIECE OF PAPER

Tony Blair signed the EU Constitution and returned from Brussels, waving his piece of paper, talking of Waterloo, presumably comparing himself to the Duke of Wellington. The truth was less impressive.

The first of Mr Blair's famous 'red lines' involved opposing a European Public Prosecutor, which his own government had earlier described as "unacceptable".

But the Constitution establishes a single European criminal code with its own prosecuting authority: Article 1.5 says, "This constitution shall have primacy over the laws of the Member States", and its provisions will "reflect existing European Court of Justice case law"... whose rulings already take precedence not only over national laws but also over national constitutions.

Britain's second 'red line' was the 'non-justiciability' of the Charter of Fundamental Rights (a provision that the Charter could not, some time in the future, be used in a court of law against us simply because we had signed the Constitution).

But on 19th June 2004 – even as the fanfares from the signing ceremony were dying away in Brussels - the senior judge at the European Court of Justice announced that he regarded the Charter as legally binding – and it is he who decides, not Mr Blair.

By now the 'red lines' have become tattered by musket-balls, the battlefield littered with discarded arms and equipment. A drifting curtain of smoke obscures the scene... Which is probably just as well, because our PM's third 'red line' was Foreign and Security policy, and here, too, our forces were outgunned and out-manoeuvred.

The text of the Constitution says: "The common foreign and security policy shall cover all aspects of foreign policy and all questions relating to the Union's security. Member states shall support the common foreign and security policy actively and unreservedly." In other words, Brussels calls the shots, and if Blair doesn't like it then he has no Marshall Blucher to come riding to the rescue.

The Prime Minister stood firm on fiscal independence for Britain, (essentially, controlling our own methods of setting interest rates and tax policy). Yet even here we are being encircled, with common EU policies on external tariffs, duty frees, tax evasion, VAT, and permissible levels of budget deficits. This is called Euro-Creep. In other words, give them enough time and they'll take that too.

On Asylum and Immigration, Mr Blair had capitulated months ago. Sir Andrew Green, Chairman of Migrationwatch UK, said of the Constitution: "This is a disaster. It locks us into a failed international convention (on refugees) and removes our autonomy in deciding how to manage an issue critical to our future."

It is hard to describe all this as a triumph of British diplomacy.

July 2004

ABNORMAL CURVATURE OF
THE FINGERS

UKIP is often accused of peddling 'Scare stories and myths about straight bananas', but these critics are either oblivious to the facts or have simply closed their minds. This is a great shame, and they do themselves a disservice.... Incidentally, the EU directive on bananas says: "They must be free from abnormal curvature of the fingers" (It's all there in 'Commission Regulation 2257, Quality Standards for Bananas')

We now face another EU farce, brought to us by Alun Michael, 'Minister for the Horse and the Quality of Urban life'. From July 2004, to comply with EU directive 93/623, all owners of horses and donkeys must have applied for a passport for each animal, at £20 (£80 for a thoroughbred horse) - with a fine of £5,000 for non-compliance.

The original idea was that anyone who ate horsemeat would be protected from ill effects of any drugs administered to the animal. But in Britain horsemeat is virtually unknown, and Westminster passed a law in 1937 forbidding the export of horses for human consumption.

As Private Eye magazine explained: "But when the EU issues a new directive, it insists it must apply to everyone. So the first consequence of the new passport scheme is that, in the name of the single market, it will now become legal to export thousands of British horses each year to furnish French and Italian dinner tables."

Apart from the cost (£18-million initially, with yearly costs of £1.5-million), most horses in France, Holland, Greece and Germany won't need passports anyway and in Eire no scheme is in place... Oh, and no fines have been set up in any other country. In Britain, of course, we've gold-plated it until it gleams. But then few Labour voters ride horses so it doesn't matter.

Alun Michael (Minister for the Horse remember, very important job) is now prating on about how useful it will be to have a "national equine database", but I ask him why? What are we going to do with it when we've got it? And what do we gain, apart from a greater empire for Mr Michael?

What is really 'asinine' is our continued membership of the EU, along with the idea that New Labour has the slightest interest in safeguarding the countryside...a countryside they clearly hate, fear, and do not understand.

July 2004

IN THE COMPANY OF WOLVES

The author George Mackay wrote in 1852: "Men, it has been well said, think in herds. It will be seen that they go mad in herds, while they only recover their senses one by one"...If so, then a critical mass of the British people seem to have recovered their senses, all thanks to Tony Blair and the European Union's detested Constitution.

On Sunday 20th June, after signing the treaty, a gaunt-looking Prime Minister appeared on BBC 1's Breakfast With Frost, and told Sir David: "The referendum will be a fascinating battle between reality and myth. The fact is that we have kept control of taxes, of our policy on immigration, of defence, of foreign policy."

This did not go down well in sections of the Labour Party. Frank Field, one of Labour's brightest and clearest-thinking MPs, was deeply unimpressed by the PM's performance: "Watching him defend the indefensible, it was Tony Blair who looked like a swivel-eyed extremist. He is saying the treaty he opposed contains nothing of importance. Even if he has from now until eternity, he will never persuade people to buy this package."

As reported by the Sun's Trevor Kavanagh (22/6/04) a group of backbench MPs have now set up Labour Against the Superstate, pledging themselves to work with UKIP and the Tories to gain a "NO" vote in the referendum... As Mr Field explained: "For 30 years voters have been fed a diet of propaganda that Britain is too weak to survive outside the EU. But they know Britain has been thriving for 12 years with unemployment half the EU average."

The group's leader, Ian Davidson, claims the support of between 80 and 100 Labour MPs, including several front-bench ministers. But as he admitted: "Being critical of a Government-supported policy isn't a career-enhancing move, and therefore people aren't going to be outing themselves at this stage."

The wolves are gathering around Tony Blair.

August 2004

GOING DUTCH

The late President Ronald Reagan was famous for his one-liners. On the budget deficit: "It's big enough to look after itself", or on his habit of taking afternoon naps: "They say hard work never killed anyone, but I figure, why take the risk?" But one of Reagan's best came during his inaugural address in 1981: "We are a nation that has a government – not the other way around."

Contrast that with the European Union in which every activity is licensed, regulated, and defined by those in Brussels, often then "gold-plated" by an army of bureaucrats in the different countries across the continent. In Britain approximately 35% of the adult workforce is now employed in the public sector (Police, Fire, Ambulance, Armed forces, HM Customs, tax and VAT inspectors, Health, and Education, not to mention the vital role played by Racial Diversity Awareness officers, Road Safety Camera Partnerships etc, etc)...all of which is a huge financial burden for the rest of the workforce who fund it.

Either we reduce that burden or we find extra money from somewhere, and one solution is withdrawal from the European Union, gaining us £30-billion a year.

The Institute of Directors gave a breakdown of the figures... The Common Agricultural Policy costs us £16-billion (half in tax, half in extra food bills), another £10-billion goes for over-regulation in all aspects of British life, and £4-billion or so in cash payments. In other words £500 per British adult, or eight times our railway budget, or £5-billion more than the defence budget. Or to put it into a local context, a mere £1-billion would build, equip, and staff for an indefinite period, one decent district hospital.

What would Ronald Reagan have made of it? Well, he would certainly have enjoyed the conclusions of a recent report from Timbro, a Swedish think-tank, which showed that if the EU were an American state it would be poorer than almost all its 50 neighbours. Not only is the EU's combined Gross Domestic Product (per capita) lower than most of the poorest states, even the richer EU countries like France, Italy, Germany are poorer than all but four states in the US.

If we move to the "heart of Europe" many British companies – already handcuffed by EU rules - will shut down. And the larger our public sector, the greater will be the impact of resulting unemployment, because the entrepreneurial spirit which creates growth and provides wealth will have been snuffed like a candle.

August 2004

IN A FLAT SPIN

The tale of the Eurofighter is a perfect example of why Britain should leave the EU. This military aircraft was developed by a consortium of UK, German, Italian, and Spanish companies. In 1985 Michael Hesiltine committed us to ordering 232 airframes, intended to combat the Soviet threat. But four years on, with the collapse of Communism, we found ourselves saddled with a vast white elephant. We should have cancelled the project and decided on a different machine, as we have done in the past, with the TSR 2 and the supersonic 1154 VTOL. But because of the EU and political pressures we were stuck with the Eurofighter.

The aircraft (renamed the Typhoon) is now ten years late, still hasn't entered service, and is £5-billion over budget and beset by technical problems. Test pilots have been told to avoid flying through clouds because computer problems risk throwing the aircraft into a "catastrophic spin". The same on-board computer also has a tendency to switch from flight mode to ground mode whilst still in the air, which might come as a shock when touching down on the heaving deck of an aircraft carrier in the middle of the Atlantic... Fortunately for the pilots, the Eurofighter/Typhoon was never designed to land on carriers. It's too heavy.

A Typhoon today will cost you £43-million, though the price will soon be tumbling, despite a total development cost of £60-million per machine...The MOD is already trying to offload fifty of them to Austria and Singapore, even before the RAF takes delivery of their first machine.

The point of all this is that technology has moved on, with 'smart missiles', combat drones, and GPS weapons' guidance systems. Also it cannot be helpful that the American Lockheed Martin F16 is a far better plane, two-thirds cheaper, and is sweeping the board on export sales.

Changing world markets have made the Eurofighter/Typhoon project unnecessary and cripplingly expensive, but it typifies the EU...the whole glazed circus marching to the beat of that distant drummer, eyes on the signpost ahead: "Cuckoo Land Around Next Bend".

August 2004

WHAT'S WRONG WITH SUET PUDDINGS?

In The Lion and the Unicorn (1941) George Orwell derided the English intelligentsia for their isolation from the common people. But not even Orwell could have reckoned how shockingly prophetic his words would become: "In intention, at any rate, the English intelligentsia are europeanised. They take their cookery from Paris and their opinions from Moscow. In the general patriotism of the country they form a sort of island of dissident thought. England is perhaps the only great country whose intellectuals are ashamed of their own nationality.

'In left-wing circles it is always felt that there is something slightly disgraceful in being an Englishman and that it is a duty to snigger at every institution, from horse racing to suet puddings...[Orwell was very fond of suet puddings]... It is a strange fact, but it is unquestionably true that almost any English intellectual would feel more ashamed of standing to attention during 'God Save the King' than of stealing from a poor box."

The rise of this curious Europeanised mind-set is responsible for the razing of the pillars upon which this nation was built. The old order is on the way out... the Church, the schools, the monarchy, the aristocracy, the set of common manners, considerations and codes of politeness that were shared by the great mass of the population.

This was nothing less than a cultural revolution. It is hard to see why any society should have tried so hard to obliterate its own history as we have done over the last few decades. But even worse is that we have replaced it with virtually nothing... an emptiness built on consumerism, apathy, and fashion; and really not much more.

September 2004

OUR COUNTRY COUSINS

You will find the spirit of bloody-minded individualism out in the countryside. As the incoming Bishop of Norwich was once told by his predecessor: "Welcome to Norfolk. If you want to lead someone in this part of the world, find out where they're going. And walk in front of them."

In the Fens, Dartmoor or the Dales, they aren't afraid to say "NO", which partly explains why New Labour hates farmers and everything they represent. They are an urban Party, born from disputes between factory owners and their workers. and simply lack the mental furniture to understand the role of the rural landscape.

Look at a few Labourites involved with Agriculture: Nick Brown, who had to borrow a pair of Wellingtons before he took up his former-Ministry, or "Lord" Larry Whitty who recently said: "The days of the small farmer are numbered." or Margaret Beckett, whose only rural link is her membership of the Caravan Club, and who, when asked by Radio 4 whether the government could do anything to help our otherwise-doomed dairy industry, replied "Not really." Thanks for that, Margaret.

Or take Ben Bradshaw, who describes farmers as "Our country cousins", and thinks that because rural houses are expensive and desirable, farmers should stop moaning and start appreciating their pleasant surroundings...With friends like these, who needs enemies?

The problem is compounded by our membership of the European Union. The whole system of the CAP works against small local producers, with French peasant farmers one of the few exceptions.

An example of the EU's dodgy attitude is the case of "Divine Chocolate", a project run by Christian Aid to help African cocoa farmers. The cocoa beans are grown in Africa, but the chocolate is made in Germany. The reason is simple: the European import levy on beans is 3%. But the import levy on manufactured chocolate is 30%. How can local African farmers compete against such a skewed system?

If I was an African cocoa farmer struggling against such restrictive practises, then I would be feeling just as bloody-minded as anyone in Norfolk.

September 2004

FORK HANDLES

You couldn't invent it... but if you did, nobody would believe you. The European Union is on the march again. This comes from EU Directive 2002/96/EC, and involves Waste Electrical and Electronic Equipment, or the WEEE Directive as they call it.

This affects everyone who manufactures, sells, distributes, or recycles electrical equipment (everything from old computers, TVs, batteries, drills, toys, electric toothbrushes etc) and - in fairness – is at least an attempt to reduce the vast amount of trash that our disposable throwaway society presently sends to landfill.

The Directive reads: "By 13th August 2005 private householders will be able to return their WEEE to collection facilities free of charge. Producers will be responsible for financing the collection, treatment, recovery, and disposal of WEEE from private households at these collection facilities. Producers will also be responsible for financing the management of WEEE from products placed on the market before 13 August 2005... The UK must have reached an average WEEE collection rate of four kilograms for each private householder annually."

Perhaps I'm imagining it, but wasn't this an old Two Ronnies sketch from 1976 or thereabouts?

October 2004

SET IN CONCRETE

My September article about the Eurofighter seems to have irritated a chap called Mr Brinley Salzmann, who dismissed my comments as half-baked and ill-informed. Sorry about this, but the facts are that this aircraft is hugely over budget, is designed to fight the wrong war, and is possibly unsafe. In fairness, it performs amazingly but technically it should not be able to fly. This is its strength and its weakness. It is kept in the air by its computer. When the computer crashes, so will the Eurofighter.

Mr Salzmann might be interested in the latest unhappy chapter of this aircraft: In an attempt to save £90 million (overall budget is now £10.5-billion and rising) the MOD took out the cannon, the bit that fires the bullets. But then they discovered that it wouldn't handle properly and the only way to restore the aerodynamics was by installing an object made of concrete into the airframe that weighed and looked the same.

Having designed their object, the MOD then realised that manufacturing costs outweighed re-fitting the original gun. So that's what they did. They refitted the original gun (£90-million remember) but to save the paltry sum of £2.5 million, they decided not to fit it with any ammunition. The Eurofighter flies without bullets

The Daily Telegraph ran this story on August 13th, where Air Commodore Andrew Lambert – one of the RAF's leading air strategists and a former commander of a fighter squadron – dismissed the notion of a fighter armed only with missiles as: "Old thinking... When you are dealing with terrorists and other unpredictable situations you want all the flexibility you can get."

What the RAF really needs, Mr Salzmann, is a cheap and cheerful ground-attack fighter that can pick out trucks in the desert. Something that we can build in Britain supporting our own aerospace industry; something that actually flies properly and fires bullets and missiles when it encounters the enemy. Something like the Jaguar that Mr Hoon is now scrapping for the disastrous Eurofighter.

October 2004

GET OFF YOUR HOSS AND DRINK YOUR MILK

Due to a recent EU directive, no 'rocking activity' toys may have a height of fall of more than 600mm. Translated into English, this means that no rocking-horse saddle shall be higher than 2ft, which threatens to put makers of traditional rocking horses out of business.

With an inevitability that is almost Athenian, it turns out that it was all a ghastly mistake.... The 600mm height was intended only to apply to outdoor horses, mounted on a spring. But thanks to standard EN71-8, this error has been published in the EU's official journal and is now considered a "harmonised standard". As a result, traditional rocking horses are now illegal.

Proof that this is not the product of my overheated imagination came in the Sun newspaper (13th Dec 2004) with the headline: "Off Their Rockers"...in which Blackie the 5-ft wooden rocking horse was removed from the cardiac unit of Alder Hey Children's Hospital in Liverpool, where he had given genuine pleasure to generations of children since 1986, without their ever having been a single reported accident.

Blackie had even been used as a logo for the 'Alder Hey Rocking Horse Appeal', raising thousands of pounds for the unit, but this counted for nothing. As a hospital spokeswoman explained: "It is an extremely large horse and parents and staff were becoming increasingly concerned about the possibility of a fall." Typically, no-one mentioned that it was all because of the EU.

Thus are we treated by the politically correct idiots who now run this land.

November 2004

SELLING ENGLAND BY THE POUND

In October 2002 a man came back from his holidays with an interesting tale to tell: "I thought you might like to hear some information I managed to extract from a (very high-ranking) civil servant who works in the Cabinet Office. I am a family man and was on holiday in the country with my family at half-term. I like a drink and I like English pubs. My wife looked after the children for a couple of hours while I went down to the local."

In the pub that evening he struck up a conversation with another drinker sitting on his own at a nearby table, nursing a glass of scotch: "He told me he was very much involved in Weights and Measures and how the government is going to get us into the euro. I quickly realised that I could get some information from this man and bought him another round. I was told that the euro/metrication issue was now so sensitive that all press releases, comments etc have to go through the Office of the Deputy Prime Minister.

'My drinking partner was working on the Metric Consolidation Bill, which will be published after the euro referendum is won, and will deal with the "confusion" then caused by the country being mostly metric. A key feature will be legislation to place all traffic and pedestrian signs in metric measurements, and motor manufacturers will be forced to change all speedometers to lead in kilometres per hour. They are also looking at regulations to ban the sale of 8oz steaks and 7" x 5" enlargements. I must admit that I was depressed after listening to him as it seems the government has got it all worked out. I hope this information is of some use to you. All I can say is "Keep up the good work". You will understand, I'm sure, if I don't give you my name.'

Before you dismiss this as conspiracy theory, please consider the following: the BBC is now part of this process of Euro-creep, with its presenters usually quoting distance-measurements in kilometres, despite the fact that here in Britain we deal in imperial miles. The National Speed Limit in Britain is 60 mph.

Another example is an HM Customs official booklet instructing anyone receiving large cash payments to comply with new anti-money laundering regulations: "The new rules apply if you deal in goods and accept payment in cash of €15,000 (about £10,000)". So even our own Customs and Excise people are quoting in euros, when the British people have made it crystal clear they wish to retain sterling.

November 2004

THE COMPLEAT TRAVELLER

Little Englanders like us are often reluctant to travel abroad. But if you must cross the Channel, you may be interested in the advice of Bulwer Wellington-Ffoulkes in his: 'THE CHANNEL CROSSING, a Guide for Travellers'.

"We British are a seafaring race, and think nothing of voyaging to foreign parts, even though it may be pretty unpleasant when we get there. The Ocean, however, has a very bad reputation with travellers, being given to typhoons, tidal waves, hammer-headed sharks, sea-serpents and the like, and you should ensure that you have a qualified captain (or, if possible, an admiral).

'Having ensured that your car is safely stowed (*well* away from the walls and other vehicles because there is always a certain amount of movement on board ship, particularly during storms) insist on being taken to the captain. Tell him to show you his credentials, and obtain answers to the following questions.

1...Are your bilges tight and in good order?

2...Are you willing to go down with your ship?

3...Will you marry me? (For use only in the event of a shipboard romance taking place).

'On request, the Purser is required to furnish you with a full passenger list and a seating plan of the lifeboats. Do not hesitate to use foul language: it is considered polite among sailors.... Ladies should remember to give the First Officer their cup size, both in inches and in centimetres, for their *brassiere de sauvetage* (lifejacket)."

I hope that this serves you well during future voyages abroad. But what a crying shame that when we crossed the Channel and joined the European Union back in the 1970s, we didn't follow Wellington-Ffoulkes' advice, and just ask the Captain a few questions beforehand.

November 2004

With thanks and acknowledgements to Tom Vernon's superb: "Fat man on a bicycle."

MUSH FOR BRAINS

In the 16th Century a band of English adventurers (including Sir Francis Drake) established a number of colonies in America. They called one of them 'Virginia', in honour of Elizabeth 1st, the Virgin Queen.

Most people already know this story, but they probably couldn't tell you Virginia's original name, which came about when a European scouting party encountered a bunch of Indians in the woods and asked them what the area was called. The locals replied: "Windgancon" and the name stuck. Only later did somebody realise that 'Windgancon' really means "What gay clothes you wear!"

You can understand why they chose to re-name the place, but at least they realised their mistake and took steps to rectify it... Unlike Defra, the government department responsible for running the countryside into the ground.

142

In 2001, during the Foot & Mouth epidemic, Defra (or MAFF if you prefer) killed 9-million healthy farm animals, but now it has a new target, a plan to slaughter and burn 23-million healthy lambs if scientists can manage to find one single sheep infected with BSE. (At one point last year they excitedly thought that they had found a link, but then it turned out that someone in the lab had muddled up the specimens and mistaken a cow's brain for a sheep's).

Under EU direction, Defra then set up the 'National Scrapie Plan' (Scrapie is a disease found in sheep, that some whiz kid decided might possibly be 'masking' BSE in sheep testing). The Plan has now been submitted to Brussels, though Britain's 70,000 sheep farmers have been given the mushroom treatment, (kept in the dark and fed on you-know -what)... The new strategy was admitted recently by Defra official Michael Beuler: if BSE is ever found in sheep, then Defra might kill every lamb in the UK, forbidding farmers from allowing their sheep to breed for two years.

When farmers asked if their lambs would be tested before being slaughtered, Defra said it would be too expensive and anyway Brussels wouldn't allow it.

So, to recap. New Labour's official policy is that they are quite happy to kill 23-million lambs, even if they are perfectly healthy, and see the collapse of Britain's sheep industry, despite the fact that there is still not one shred of proof that eating BSE -infected beef leads to CJD in humans. In fact, as CJD figures continue to decline, the evidence seems to confirm that such a link never existed.

Unfortunately Defra – renowned for its perceived lack of acquaintance with the higher mental processes - is unlikely to be troubled by anything so mundane as a lack of evidence.

December 2004

PETER MANDELSON,
TILLY THE TERRIER,
AND AN UNMADE BED (don't ask)

It's a very odd world... Tony Blair appoints Peter
Mandelson as an EU commissioner, presumably in the
belief that he will help the euro cause, (but if Blair is
proved right, then I'm Judith Chalmers)...while
Chancellor Gordon Brown responds to all those
Council Tax rebels by putting bills UP not DOWN for
most people who live in their own house... the one
they have spent years buying, using hard-earned
income that has already been taxed by the Inland
Revenue.

A good solution for home-owners is to deliberately
lower the value of their own house - dropping it down
through the tax bands, thus saving money - and a
BBC Radio 4 programme recently asked listeners to
suggest the easiest methods. They asked the question:
"What is the worst thing you have ever seen in a
house?" (i.e.: brown and salmon-pink bathroom suite,
or plastic windows in a Georgian rectory), but they got
some unexpected answers. One person said,
"Children"; another said, "The river Medway", and a
third said: "The psychiatric nurse I'd been avoiding all
week." As I say: a very strange world

If you're still not convinced, may I present Tilly the
Jack Russell terrier, who lives in Chicago and is
making a name for herself as an artist. She scratches
around on wet canvas, biting, rolling, and generally
'worrying' the paint. Her work has just appeared in a
one-dog exhibition in New York, and is selling like hot
bonios in Germany, Japan and the Netherlands...Tilly
begins by gnawing along the edge of the canvas, a
metaphor for the fact that she is on the fringes of the
art world.

But Tilly might be nearer the mainstream than she realises: The artist (sorry, 'art's practitioner') Tracey Emin struck gold a few years ago with her exhibit: Unmade Bed. Speaking personally I've always had the urge to visit her studio, plump up the pillows, brush out the fag ends and biscuit crumbs, and straighten the duvet. I realise the fault is all mine, probably some childhood trauma...but in this crazy circus of Tilly the Terrier and Peter Mandelson, I wonder: is *anything* really odd anymore?

December 2004

HO, HO. HO!

Every year, in December, the Royal Mail intercepts hundreds of items addressed to Father Christmas. At one Sorting Office the manager found a letter written by an old man who lived alone, asking Santa for five pounds to give himself a festive treat. The supervisor was very touched by this, so he pinned the letter to a notice board alongside a small collection tin. By the end of the shift the contributions amounted to £3.43p, so he made it up to £4.00 from his own pocket and sent off four pound notes to the old chap, with the compliments of Father Christmas.

By return of post he received a reply: "Dear Santa, thank you very much for the £4.00 – but I reckon those thieving gits at the Post Office must have nicked one of the notes".

Well, I'm afraid the European Union has gone one better, and stolen our entire postal system. Before the EU came along, the Post Office was that rare and unique thing: a State-owned monopoly that actually made a profit, even contributing cash to the Treasury.

The service even had elements of a social service by maintaining some post offices and collections/deliveries where (in all honesty) they might not be profitable. But overall, a benefit was continued to the community as a whole. A letter delivered in London helped subsidise one delivered to the Orkneys.

As a result of EU laws (splitting it up into Parcelforce, Counters, and Royal Mail Letters) the entire industry was "modernised", and "liberalised" and firms like DHL, TNT, and the heavily-subsidised German Post Office, all moved in and cherry-picked the profitable areas in cities or on good travel networks, leaving the poor old Post Office with the scrag-end. And when you're left with the unprofitable parts, you have to get rid of the most expensive elements or you go totally bust, which is why hundreds of rural and urban post offices have already drawn down the shutters, leaving thousands of people - many of them elderly or infirm - with no local service.

EU Directive 97/67/EC is doing to our whole postal system what Directive 91/440 did to our railways. It's probably too late now for the Post Office, unless we leave the EU and start again. But the ultimate insult has to be when Labour politicians start protesting against Post Office closures, when the final nail in the coffin was their own Government's decision to withdraw pensions and TV licences from post offices. To my mind, given Labour's unswerving loyalty to the disastrous Grand European Project, such hypocrisy is utterly unforgivable.

December 2004

2005

THE CHARLEMAGNE OLYMPICS

Now that the dust has settled over the 2004 Athens Olympics, you might like to know that the overall winner was the European Union. As reported by the Sun's Trevor Kavanagh (31/8/04), Romano Prodi, the out-going EU President, hailed Britain's haul of gold medals as a triumph for the European Union...

Mr Prodi said: "The Games were a huge success thanks to their unique spirit and smooth organisation but also because EU athletes did so well. In 2008 I hope to see the teams in Beijing carry the flag of the European Union alongside their own national flag as a symbol of our unity... The EU's sportsmen and women performed outstandingly at Athens, winning 82 gold medals and more than 280 in total."

Unfortunately this dimwit is not alone: Ingo Friedrich, German vice-president of the Euro Parliament insisted that medals must be listed under the EU to "foster a European identity", and Commission spokesman Reijo Kemppinen claimed: "The EU swept the floor at the Olympic Games."

As the Sun commentated: "They just don't get it in Brussels, do they? When it comes to sport- and so many other things – we're not all on the same side and never will be. People like Kelly Holmes, Amir Kahn, our rowers and the men's relay team were competing for Britain, not the EU... Don't be tempted to brush aside Prodi's daft ideas as a joke. Like all those who run the EU, he is a dangerous megalomaniac whose aim is a European superstate."

January 2005

BEATEN WITH THE UGLY STICK

The New Economics Foundation reported in August 2004 that many of Britain's historic town-centres have become identikits of each other; mass-produced clones, soulless and lifeless. Look down most High Streets and the proof is self-evident...a vista of Dorothy Perkins, W.H. Smith, Blockbuster, and McDonald's. Very few of our old towns have survived (though I'd like to nominate Sidmouth and Ashburton as Devon contenders). Elsewhere, the old buildings have either been bulldozed or had their wonderful old frontages ripped out in favour of plate-glass and corporate logos... And it is ugly, ugly, ugly.

As Walter Gropius once wrote: "Can a child growing up in Main Street be expected to be in the habit of looking for beauty? He hasn't met with it yet and wouldn't recognise it because his perceptive faculties have been blunted by the ruthless assault of the chaotic colours, shapes and noises."

The most obvious casualties of this vandalism were the small independent shops in the cities, many of which were driven out; only the charity shops could survive. But the consequences also reached into the countryside.

Take the little Devon village of Exbourne. In 1851 there were three thatchers, two butchers, two bakers, a grocer, a blacksmith, a cobbler, a postmaster, two innkeepers, one haberdasher, and a poultry dealer, plus numerous local craftsmen and farmers. Thirty years ago there were over 20 outlets for milk in the Exbourne Parish, mostly supplying the Ambrosia factory. Today there is not a single one. Not one. They have all gone. The cow-sheds lie weed-choked and empty, the converted barns forming a picturesque backdrop for the new owner's Porsche. The last few surviving farmers have abandoned milk production

As for Exbourne village itself, there is now one pub, a garage, and a small business maintaining agricultural and garden machinery. The other "amenities" have all disappeared. The last bakery closed in 1982, having operated since the 19th Century. The school is one of the smallest in Devon, and its survival is a minor miracle.

We all know that the sepia-tinted idyll of blacksmith and cobbler has gone forever; but we can rebuild much of what has been lost. And one of the main platforms for that is the farming industry, the thing the countryside does best. If we lose our farmers then the entire country is in trouble. Big trouble.

January 2005

"GO GIT A PROPER JOB"

Next time somebody tells you they want to abolish the House of Lords, perhaps they might be interested in the official figures released by Parliament, detailing the costs of running Westminster.

Peers of the Realm, do not, of course, receive a salary, but they do get a small daily attendance allowance. Here are the figures for 2003-4; though before we proceed you may wish to fix yourself a stiff brandy and adopt a reclining position, just to be on the safe side.

Total cost for the Lords is £61-million. For the House of Commons, £269-million. And for the European Parliament (the MEPs) £90-million. Even more interesting (and you may find yourself reaching for the bottle after this) the total costs per member were as follows: House of Lords: £91,000...House of Commons: £409,000...and the European Parliament a whopping £1,138,000.

In the 2002-3 session, the EU Parliament sat 161 days, the House of Commons 162 days, and the House of Lords 174 days. You don't need to be an economic wizard to notice that something is very wrong here, particularly when we know that the EU is so riddled with corruption and financial irregularity that they sacked their own chief accountant when she refused to approve their crooked accounts. As Sir Lew Grade once remarked about his movie Raise the Titanic: "It would have been cheaper to lower the Atlantic" (though I prefer the comment of one of the passengers on the ill-fated ship: "I know I ordered ice with my Gordons but this is ridiculous")

The EU not only resembles a doomed liner, impossible to turn around, but this empty vessel is costing us a fortune.

January 2005

A COMMON RESOURCE

Out in the grey heaving wastes of the Irish Sea, aboard the 23-metre trawler 'Kiroan', at 5'o clock in the morning, skipper Philip Dell prepared to land two nets bulging with fish. In the glare of floodlights he swung them across to the stern hatchway, where they cascaded down onto the conveyor belt below; thousands of tiny plaice, three-inches long, flapping and gasping in their death throes.

The crew were being observed by Tory Shadow fisheries minister, Owen Paterson, who said: "We watched in horror as the crew swept the undersize fish along the belt, flushing them through an opening in the hull, back into the sea...We estimated that 90% of the catch was dumped".

The second net was larger... with mostly dogfish this time, unsaleable and unwanted, and they, too, went along the belt. Mr Paterson again: "Plunging into the water, each shook themselves, as if indignant of their treatment, and swam away, none the worst".

There are two net-sizes: 80mm and 110mm. Our fishermen are forced to use 80mm nets in order to placate the Belgian fleet (the Belgians are after sole, which slip through the larger size). But these smaller nets also scoop up next year's harvest, the young fish.

Skipper Phillip Dell explained to his visitors down in the tiny mess-room, sipping hot tea as they braced themselves against the pitching of the boat: In 1984 the Fleetwood fleet numbered seventy vessels. Now there are only seven; and Mr Dell is allowed only 22 days at sea. If he uses the larger 110mm nets (his preference, the one used to catch the dogfish mentioned above) EU rules restrict him to 17 days at sea, which would drive him out of business and send his crew to the dole office.

Mr Patterson again: 'Standing in front of us as we sat in that tiny room Dell spoke with a passion born of frustration and outrage, the outrage of a professional fisherman forced to do something he knew to be wrong.'

"It needs stopping", said Dell, "We've been doing this for ten months and we're slaughtering the fish"

When Ben Bradshaw, fisheries minister, swept up from London, Dell asked him to explain the policy. "He couldn't...He just asked an aide to jot down the details. We never heard from him again", Dell added bitterly.

As for those Belgian beam trawlers, they drag huge 12-metre trawls at an amazing 7-knots, hoovering everything from the seabed, raking up the sand and mud to get at the buried sole.

"We've followed up behind them," said Dell, "and everything is dead. The ultimate irony is that in following sole the Belgians have a by-catch of protected cod, which they dump overboard so that it is not declared. They don't even want the fish."

January 2005

With acknowledgements to Ian Bookless, Country Illustrated Magazine

THE HIGHWAY CODE

In August 2002 six-year-old Daniel Hennessy went with his Mum to buy some sweets from a corner shop in Manchester. He never made it there. A teenaged joyrider named Sajid Hussain ran over him in a stolen car and left him for dead. Daniel's world was destroyed that day and he is now confined to a wheelchair, paralysed from the chest down.

Hussain (I have a Daily Mail photograph of this gentleman, turning to give the camera a charming gesture involving two upraised fingers) was banned from driving for two years.... Now call me picky, but if this is justice then I am Captain Scott. True, Hussain is now behind bars, serving 18-months, but for running down a lollipop lady **six months after** crippling little Daniel. How can any society function when the criminal system is so blatantly unfair, unjust and utterly useless?

Daniel's story is tragic, but Kathryn Austin's enters Monty Python Land. Her Ford Fiesta was stolen from outside her father's house in Exeter, so she reported it missing. A few days later she spotted it driving around the city and discreetly followed, calling the Police on her mobile. A squad car arrived – blue lights flashing - but abandoned the chase when the stolen vehicle jumped a red light and drove away at 50mph (this was late at night with virtually no other traffic in the area).

The Fiesta was later found abandoned, so the Police took it to the pound at Cullompton to test for fingerprints. They found none, so that was that. Except that Mrs Austin was informed that she now owed them £117 for storage costs...for her own car!

Is this what we pay our taxes for? You work it out...Mrs Austin couldn't, and in all honesty neither can I.

January 2005

THE SUN SAYS

This comes from The Sun...and jolly interesting it is, too, in a sort of "appalled fascination" kind of way. It's a report on fraud and corruption in Brussels (21/7/04) and it involves you directly because it is your hard-earned money they're spending.

THE SUN SAYS: "In Brussels they don't spend money like water. They spend it like champagne. There cannot be an empire anywhere in the world that is such a hot-bed of greed, corruption and waste as the European Union...By the time the 2009 session ends UK taxpayers will have pumped £32.5-billion into the bloated monster...Even the EU's own fraudbusters reckon that in the year ending June 2003 the proven scams cost it a staggering £590 million. The real figure is feared to be far higher."

The newspaper then lists a number of fraud cases, including an EU lawyer who claimed expenses "for a total number of working days in excess of actual working days possible.", and another convicted of forgery, fraud, and deception after creating false travel documents to support her claims for attending meetings that were never held.

And such waste is built into the system, because the EU has THREE headquarters, and once a month a convoy of lorries makes the 434-mile round trip shuttling between Brussels and Strasbourg at a cost of £70-million a year.

Most ironical of all is that the EU's Anti Corruption Czar, Neil Kinnock, was also responsible for the fiasco of the 13-storey Berlaymont building in Brussels. Mr Kinnock paid a total of £800-million for these dilapidated offices which have been unusable for 13 years.

Senior EU official Didier Hespel explained one of the reasons for the delay: "It could take up to six weeks for a question on lightbulb specifications and another six weeks for the answer to get back...The saga of the Berleymont building has been with us more than ten years, to such an extent that none of the people who started work on it are associated with the project today".

The star-shaped concrete and glass building was

intended as the EU's answer to the US White House, but as Tory MEP Chris Heaton-Harris told the Sun: "It just typifies Europe. It is an expensive, useless white elephant."

Personally I agree totally with him, but we can't reform this behemoth from within; and the sooner the Conservatives admit it, the better for everyone.

February 2005

UP AS WELL AS DOWN

If you are tempted by a "Euro-Mortgage", then please STOP for just a moment, clear a space on the tabletop, and bang your forehead smartly a couple of times... Now then, doesn't that feel better? (A small pain now, rather than a huge one later...See how I look after you?).

Euro-Mortgages were announced in December 2004. The "Forum on Mortgage Credit" in Brussels claimed that an effective single market could mean cheaper loans for all, which sounds splendid until you look at the small print. Mike Warburton, senior partner at accountants Grant Thornton, responded: "It's bad practice for somebody to have a mortgage in a currency other than the currency they are buying the property in, or if you are somebody who doesn't work part of your time overseas."

If you had bought a house with a euro mortgage two years ago that mortgage would now be 10% more expensive, thanks to currency fluctuations. As Mr Warburton said: "To get a mortgage in euros on a house in Britain is just madness. You might as well put your money on the 3.30 at Epsom" (Daily Telegraph 14/12/04).

But there is another aspect to this. If Britain signs up to EU-wide mortgages we would lose the power to change interest rates, which we need for cooling down the housing market and consumer spending when they threaten to get out of control. A single market for mortgages...and other forms of lending would certainly follow...will deprive even non-euro members like ourselves of control over monetary policy.

In other words, the European Central Bank will have sent their tanks around to the back door, while we were defending the Maginot Line in the front garden. The case for keeping Sterling would be badly undermined..."After all," as Peter Mandelson would doubtless point out, "why defend the £ if all loans are in Euros?"

March 2005

"YOUR PAPERS"

How sadly predictable that the Conservatives have backed Labour's plans to issue us all with ID cards. The UK Independence Party is totally opposed to these cards. They are expensive, intrusive, and doomed to fail in catching crooks and terrorists. Even Lady Thatcher describes them as: "A Germanic concept, completely alien to this country."

There are some 250,000 failed asylum seekers hiding somewhere in Britain. If they can acquire a false identity (which doesn't seem that difficult these days) they can use the ID card to become legal. As it is, anyone entering the UK on holiday/business won't need a card anyway, so it won't stop Bin Laden or the Russian Mafia. ID cards are needed so urgently that they won't even be widely available until 2012, though from 2007 new passport applicants will be forced to purchase one at a charge of £43.

It will cost an estimated £3billion to get the scheme working, but the real costs are bound to be far greater. And for what? To make us one of the most snooped-upon nations on earth, from cot to coffin.

David Blunkett once likened ID cards to a Tesco 'Clubcard', but they are far worse than that, with every possible scrap of information going to a database available to all government departments and quangoes. Besides, loyalty cards are voluntary, and although they might track your spending, they do not contain details of your medical history, religious beliefs, political affiliations, income, occupation, personal finances, or DNA.

In time the ID card will contain all this information and more; and all those people who say, "Well, if you've got something to hide..." will soon have their way. You really will have nothing left to hide, because the state will know it all already. And if the state ever turned into a dictatorship, you would have nowhere left to hide either.

Please look at it this way. If I quizzed you on your personal details you would rightly tell me to mind my own business. So why on earth allow the Government – the government, for heaven's sake, especially this government – to gather all this information on you? And the Tories - displaying all the adroitness of a hippo in the goalmouth - have now gone along with it. This country is screaming out for a new government ...and right now little UKIP looks the best long-term bet.

March 2005

DIVERSIFY, DIVERSIFY

John Widdecombe is a small dairy farmer from South Brent in Devon. In a heart-breaking letter to the Daily Telegraph last summer, he described his plight. His milk was selling for the lowest price in Europe (7p a pint), and he was working for 80-90 hours a week, supplementing his income by labouring on a building site (this is presumably what New Labour means by "diversifying").

Under the EU quota system we are forced to import 15% of our milk and milk products, though we could easily supply 100% of our domestic needs. If a British farmer exceeds their allowance of milk, they cannot simply pour the surplus onto the land or down the nearest drain because the authorities would jump on them like a ton of bricks.

In the words of the comedian Jethro: "See, what 'appened was...". Nationally Britain went 0.17% over its milk quota for the first time in many years, so the EU fined us £5.8 million (that alone sticks in my craw) but the Government then shovelled the bill onto the dairy farmers. No problem there, because most farmers don't vote Labour.

As for poor Mr Widdecombe on his farm in South Brent, he was presented with a £42,000 bill from Defra, and his plans for bringing his son into the business were thrown into jeopardy.

With 61-years now being the average age of a British dairy farmer, with scores of them selling up every week, we need to encourage young people (preferably from farming backgrounds) to join the industry. Britain needs farmers...it's as simple as that. We need control over our own food output, and wherever possible that food must be fresh and locally produced.

Or do you want all your chickens to come from Thailand?

March 2005

BROTHER "CHE" FOR SAINTHOOD

The T&G "Record" is the official newspaper of the Transport & General Workers' Union, circulated to all its members. In the November 2004 edition Old Socialism is still alive and kicking. There's a report from the 2004 TUC Conference with Jack Dromey demanding: "A mandatory obligation on all employers to provide and contribute towards a decent occupational pension" (for all their workforce)...this in addition to all the extra EU costs that have been lumped onto business people, not to mention Gordon Brown's £6-billion raid on pension funds which then caused a collapse of the whole pensions industry, despite the fact that he'd already been warned not to do it beforehand.

Back to Comrade Dromey, who also wants to see an increase in migrant workers to Britain: "Our message today to migrant workers is", he tells the Conference, "you are welcome to our shores in search of a better life". Presumably they will all join the T&G, and contribute to Mr Dromey's pension fund, though I wonder if all these migrant workers will need biometric ID cards?

Worst of all is a glowing report on the opening of the European Social Forum, held at Southwark Cathedral, in London, attended by at least 25,000 trade unionists. Among the speakers were Gerry Adams (IRA etc) and Aleida Guevara, daughter of Che Guevara, the hardline Marxist revolutionary who summarily executed more than 50 people following the Cuban revolution, before Castro reined him in, and who as head of both the Central Bank and industrial production was an utter disaster...though he proved jolly handy at exporting revolution throughout South America. "Elections", he once asked a human rights activist, "Whatever for?"

Che Guevara admired the Chinese Cultural Revolution and increasingly called for "a daily quota of death and suffering", demanding that the oppressed peoples of Latin America should suffer more, so that they would stop believing in peaceful democratic change.

It strikes me that if the T&G wishes to be seen as a moderate mature organisation, working in partnership with employers (who pay their salaries, after all) they really need to grow up a little, and stop fighting ideological battles from their teenage years.

April 2005

ENEMY AT THE GATE

May I share with you a few lines from the book 'News From Somewhere', by Professor Roger Scruton, on the subject of farming: "When wet and warm the land is heaven to the herds. When wet and cold it is hell. In mid-October their attitude suddenly changes, and there they are each morning at the gate, begging to come in. This is the moment when the bond between farmer and herd is finally sealed – when the reality of the farm, as a homestead, a shelter, a place of cohabitation and concord, is finally acknowledged by both sides to the contract. There is something ineffably soothing about the quiet stable of horses, the barn filled with the gentle shuffling of cows."

Professor Scruton claims that the animals come to accept the farmer as their necessary provider: "It could be that this experience of oneness with protected animals is the true reason why people stay farming...The farmer is not merely living in a particular place, but dwelling there, sovereign over the herd, and belonging where they belong...That is why, when a livestock farmer can no longer make ends meet, he does not sell up and join the dole queue in the city. He nods goodbye to his herd, then turns away and shoots himself."

When Britain's livestock industry has been reduced to a handful of farms catering to the top end of the market, and the EU has made us totally dependant on foreign imports of dubious quality, somebody may one day have the novel idea of Britain starting its own breeding programme for livestock. "Home-Reared Meat" they will call it.

But they will face one major problem...all the skills and knowledge, passed on, down through generations of farmers, will have been lost, totally beyond recovery.

April 2005

BRING BACK HATTIE JACQUES

In the National Health Service superbugs like MRSA kill more people every year (5,000 or so) than die on Britain's roads. In the face of this, New Labour is like a rabbit in the headlights, transfixed, mesmerised, powerless....

Clair Rayner, agony aunt and former nurse, writing in the Guardian in 2004, was in no doubt: "We worked incredibly hard to keep our hospital clean...we scrubbed everything. When a patient was discharged, the bed was scourged from top to bottom, including the mattress, to make it fit for the next patient. And we scrubbed ourselves too. We washed our hands 40 or more times a day. We changed our uniforms if the slightest smear of blood or other bodily fluid marked it. We *NEVER LEFT THE HOSPITAL IN UNIFORM*, [my italics] never wore make-up and had to manicure our fingernails every week, without polish...And we never had any cross infection between patients".

But now MRSA infects virtually every hospital in the land; and patients (and some visitors) are terrified of even a brief stay on the wards. One example of this...a friend of mine recently saw a consultant-surgeon about a minor operation. He asked: "Will I have to stay in overnight?" to which the consultant replied, "Good God, no. We want you to come out alive."

UKIP's cure for hospital superbugs is the return of a 'Matron' with the clout and independence to rule (and we mean RULE) the wards with authority and discipline. We also need to encourage older, possibly retired nurses back into the profession, possibly as ward sisters, to educate the younger medical staff with a few basic lessons in ward hygiene.

I'm not blaming the younger staff; clearly there is a problem with how they were taught, but when even qualified doctors wander around the wards, out of uniform, munching on snacks and fizzy drinks, something has gone wrong. The UK Independence Party will put this right. And that is a promise.

May 2005

164

RED HERRING IN A STEEL CONSTITUENCY

Denis MacShane is our Europe Minister...at the moment. Though Tony Blair might well have opened the trapdoor beneath him by the time you read this.

In a December 2004 speech to students at Durham University, he said: "Europe is very young. This treaty [the EU Constitution] won't be the last word". But he had told the Western Morning News on 4th June 2002 that the Constitution would: "settle for a generation the question of how Europe is run", which rather undermines No 10's claim that the Constitution is a final step intended to limit the EU's powers.

MacShane revealed to those Durham students that Gordon Brown's 5-tests for the euro were: "A giant red herring". But when challenged on this he spluttered: "Jesus Christ, no. 'Red herring' is not one of my favourite metaphors". Which he then retracted when the Scotsman newspaper (4th December) produced a tape recording of the speech.

On 9th December, he told the New Statesman he'd always been against joining the euro: "For F***k's sake, the euro. This really drives me mad. I represent a steel constituency. Under no circumstances would I have voted in the first 4 or 5 years of the Labour Government, at the rate the pound was at against the euro, to go into the currency."

But three years earlier, on 2nd Feb 2001, he told the Financial Times: "The folly of pretending the relationship of our currency with the rest of the EU does not matter, is now exposed in terms of thousands of lost steel jobs."

If you still feel that this gentleman is familiar with the notion of having principles and sticking by them, then consider this. In his December interview with the New Statesman the Minister claimed that he had been in favour of a referendum on the Constitution all along. He told them: "I don't remember a single statement by a pro-European that we shouldn't have a referendum".... But in June 2003 (recorded in Hansard) he told the House of Commons: "It is parliament that should decide the affairs of our British people, not populist plebiscites".

If you are deeply, deeply unimpressed by Mr MacShane then – to put it mildly – that makes an absolute minimum of two of us.

May 2005

IN THE BAR WITH BRONSON

Charles Bronson (not the film actor) was jailed for seven years in 1974 after robbing a Liverpool jeweller of £35. Since then, 25 years have been added to his sentence - 22 of them spent in solitary confinement. During his prison career he has led eight rooftop protests, assaulted 20 warders, taken hostage two governors and seven Iraqi terrorists, and lassoed a visiting teacher with a skipping rope. According to "Brewer's Gallery of Rogues" he also likes to demonstrate his great strength by bending the bars on his cell door and performing 2,000 press-ups with a prison officer on his back.

Mr Bronson certainly deserved to go to prison but the fact remains that this is the law of Unintended Consequences in action. Rather like the European Union.

When we originally joined the Common Market it was

sold to us as a trading arrangement. To many it made sense to remove tariffs and other trade barriers, and encourage ease of travel throughout Europe. But if you look in more detail it's now clear that the politicians knew exactly where it led - to a country called Europe.

For those who STILL support our membership of the EU, and would vote 'Yes' in a referendum on the Constitution, they at least have the advantage of hindsight and can see where the EU is heading. They cannot use the excuse: "We didn't realise. Nobody told us". And if with their help Britain is ever daft enough to vote 'Yes' then the cell door really will have clanged shut behind us.

May 2005

THE BRAIN OF POOH

Last year a lady named Jane Howell, in various newspapers, accused this column of misunderstanding the European Union, which she described as a 'bold project', adding: "We should not assume that the UK, France or Germany are relinquishing their rights as a nation...UKIP assumes that because bears are big, brown and hairy, therefore everything that is big, brown and hairy must be a bear."

I thank Ms Howell for her information on bears, but may I quote Giscard d'Estaing, who chaired all the negotiations on the EU Constitution. In a speech in Aachen, Germany, in May 2003, he said: "Our constitution cannot be reduced to a mere treaty for co-operation between governments. Anyone who has not yet grasped this fact deserves to wear the dunce's cap...Our continent has seen successive attempts at unifying it: Ceasar, Charlemagne, and Napoleon among others. We seek to unify it by the pen, where the sword has finally failed."

As for bears, if I'm out walking in the woods – in bear country – and a big, brown hairy animal - eight feet tall – springs out at me and roars, giving me the benefit of its halitosis, I will naturally assume "Bear".

And if someone hiding up a tree then shouts down: "Relax. It's not a bear. It's the Vicar in fancy dress, out fund-raising for the new church roof", then I will treat this with scepticism.

To misquote Dr Johnson: If it looks like a bear, walks and smells like a bear, and growls "I am a bear" in a big deep, gravelly voice that sounds like a bear, then it's a bear... It's a bear, Ms Howell, and a big one.

May 2005

[with thanks to Godfrey Bloom MEP]

SOIL AND SENSIBILITY

The European Union has decreed that Britain's green and pleasant land is to be stripped of livestock production. The future for our countryside is to be either a tourist leisure park, or for the production of arable crops, to be used as bio-fuel... In mid-Devon at this very moment the residents of Winkleigh are fighting plans for a biomass power station, which will probably wreck the village. The bigger problem is that the EU's plans will wreck what's left of the entire countryside

The reason is simple and it comes from the part of an animal which is farthest from its nose. Grass is eaten at the front, and manure falls onto the ground from the rear, which generates the humus to maintain soil fertility.

In India they began to burn cow manure for fuel instead of digging it into the land. With no humus in the soil the winds and rain soon eroded away the topsoil. The crops then failed and famine ensued.

Rural motorists reading this must have noticed two things: the fields being virtually empty of animals, and in wet weather the amount of discoloured water now collecting across the roadway. This is caused partly by new building on flood plains, but mainly by the huge increase in ploughed fields. Heavy rain just washes straight off cultivated land, taking soil and nutrients with it; but a field of grass acts like a sponge, soaking up excessive rainfall and easing problems of flooding.

For the sake of our countryside we need animals in the fields – preferably ones we can eat. Under the EU's plans we are destined to lose our livestock heritage and witness our fields literally wash away in front of our eyes.

June 2007

MR ED SPEAKS OUT

Every so often, from various sources, I come across quotes from people who really know about what is happening with the European Union...often because they are responsible for making it happen in the first place. Rather than drip-feeding them to you, it's probably far quicker to pass them onto you straight from the horse's mouth and let you decide for yourselves. So here are a few of them.

"In order to unify Europe it is first of all necessary to wrest power out of your hands. We will do it. We will unite Europe. National autonomy no longer suffices. Economic devolution demands the abolition of national frontiers. If Europe is to remain split into national groups then capitalism will recommence its work. Only a Federated Republic of Europe can give peace to the world" (Trotsky in 1929).

Or how about this one, which is honest at least: "The Constitution is more than just a milestone. I think it is the birth certificate of the United States of Europe. It is not the end point of integration but the framework for – as it says in the preamble (the introduction) – an ever closer union". (Hans Martin Bury, German Europe Minister).

Or you might prefer this lengthy one, from Miguel Moratinos, the Socialist Spanish foreign minister: "Britain's days as an independent country will soon be over. We are witnessing the last remnants of national politics."

And when asked if the Constitution would strip national parliaments such as Westminster of their powers, he said: "Absolutely. They have already signed away power to run their own economy, legal system and human rights rules. The next step will be to form a Europe-wide foreign policy and merge the armed forces into a single European army. The member states have already relinquished control of justice, liberty and security. The difficult part is approaching – the giving up of sovereignty in the dual arenas of foreign affairs and defence. The concept of traditional citizenship has been by-passed in the 21st Century.

Patriotism will be swept away as we all become Europeans."

And if the above doesn't worry you, nothing will.

July 2005

ONE DAY WITH DAISY

In late-2003 the Tenant Farmers Association wanted to publish a small glossy magazine, advertising their produce in a £1m campaign. So they applied to DEFRA for a £300,000 grant under the Rural Enterprise Scheme - But that's where it all started to go pear-shaped.

Jeremy Cowper, senior Defra official, studied a dummy version of the magazine and in March 2005 (18 months later) rejected the application, explaining: "Many of the proposed articles would breach article 28 of the Treaty (of Rome) because of their focus on the British origin of the product".

Mr Cowper didn't like the cover story: "One Day With Daisy", which described three city executives trying their hand at milking a cow, claiming that a picture of Jersey cows in rolling green fields was too British: "Lots of pictures of an obviously British landscape would add to the overall focus on origin and could tip the balance."

Another article troubling Mr Cowper concerned a Leicestershire farmer who spent his holidays digging a pond. The pictures included a kingfisher, a JCB digger, and the offending pond. Too British again. If only the photographer had snapped a few poplar trees, an olive grove, a distant view of the Eiffel Tower.

Cowper also objected to a feature on favourite regional dishes of media personalities such as Mark Lamarr, Sean Bean and Fay Weldon. Mr Cowper (towards whom I now have the sort of uncharitable feelings that shouldn't go into print) ruled that these could only comply with Brussels rules if the magazine was not distributed in the particular regions concerned, which rather undermines much of the marketing strategy behind the whole enterprise.

With depressing predictability an article about barbecues was criticised for suggesting that "British is Best", and therefore in breach of Article 28 of the Treaty of Rome, and as a result – to quote Defra – "The combined effect of the magazine would breach article 28 [and 20] regarding advertising of home market-based products, and is therefore ineligible for Rural Enterprise Scheme funds".

Read the above, and weep for a country that used to run an empire, and is now run by a commission of clowns.

July 2005

WHERE'S THE DAILY MIRROR?

I realise that it's old hat now, but I can't resist mentioning the euro (not that we'll be joining it for a while). Three EU countries - Sweden, Denmark and the UK - said "No thanks" to the Single Currency. All three are doing much better as a result.

Italy, in marked contrast, is on her knees, and HSBC – one of the world's largest banks – has said that Rome would be better off returning to the Lira. Even more significantly, EU Monetary Commissioner Joaquin Amunia has recently admitted to doubts over whether

Italy can survive inside the Eurozone. This is like the Pope telling Richard and Judy that he's not sure whether that bloke God exists.

Continuing the spiritual theme it has been said that there is much joy in Heaven when one sinner repenteth, so they must have had a humdinger of a party upstairs when the Swedish newspaper Expressen (which had campaigned strongly for the euro in the 2003 referendum) admitted that it had been wrong and the Swedish people had, after all, been right.

As Expressen said: "The real Swedish economy consists of many people who work, pay their mortgages, and try to live off their pensions, and if most of them find that they do not need the euro, they may be right".

Better late than never. All we need now is for the Daily Mirror to come on side and we're sorted.

July 2005

But see page 176 about Britain still getting the euro

SINGLE CURRENCY?

Two things will have happened by the time you read this. Either Italy will be near to crashing out of the euro (unlikely) or some savage arm-twisting will have occurred between Brussels and Rome (very likely).

In May 2005 the German magazine "Stern" advised it readers to check their euro notes very carefully. German-issued notes, they explained, have serial numbers beginning with an "X", so hold onto those. On the other hand, the Italian notes begin with an "S"

- this was news to me, too - and you should get rid of them at once.

The reason was that recession-hit Italy could soon be forced to pull out of the Single Currency because they have lost their ability to set interest rates and decide their own taxation and spending (thus losing control of their own economy) and "Stern" didn't want its German readers left holding a lot of redundant toy money.

The Italians themselves, are painfully aware of their plight. Unemployment is high, wage demands are increasing, and the Rome government is deeply in the red. Roberto Maroni, welfare minister, was asked whether Italy should ditch the euro: "We should not disregard this hypothesis because it is not impossible. Shouldn't it be better to go back, temporarily to a system with double currencies? In Europe, there is one perfect example. Great Britain, which grows and develops while maintaining its own currency." (Daily Telegraph, 04/06/05)

It probably won't happen. Following the rejection of the EU Constitution, and the vitriolic deadlock between Chirac and Tony Blair at the recent budget talks, for Italy to then pull out of the euro would see utter pandemonium in Brussels, with the place collapsing like a pack of cards. But let's hope that I'm wrong. Let's hope that Rome makes the right decision.

July 2005

(I was right, and Rome didn't)

NO BUT YES, BUT NO BUT YES, BUT NO BUT...

When does "No" mean "Yes"? The answer's easy: whenever the EU is involved.

Do you remember France and the Netherlands voting "No" to the EU Constitution? Well, that counted for nothing. Brussels is building a United States of Europe, and a silly little thing like public opinion is irrelevant.

You seek proof? Of course you do. Jean Claude Juncker, the President of 'Europe' said after the referendum: "I really believe that the French and Dutch did not vote no to the constitutional treaty."

Valery Giscard d'Estaing, the man who drafted the Constitution, even came out with the classic line: "It is not possible for anyone to understand the full text". As journalist Mark Steyn observed: 'Europe's Jefferson has become its Jefferson Airplane, boasting about the impenetrability of his own drug-induced lyrics.'

One thing is crystal clear, although the British People will say no to any EU Constitution, they are already being out-manoeuvred. Brussels is even now bringing in many things that were in the original document: an EU diplomatic service, Euro defence agency, Euro Space Agency, Common Asylum and Immigration policy, Rapid Reaction Force, Fundamental Rights Agency, Euro Gendarmerie, and EU president and foreign minister, among many other things.

So there you have it. In Brussels "No" means "Yes", even when it means "No". What I find intriguing is that when it's a "Yes" (like the Spanish "Yes" vote in the referendum) that isn't considered as a "No".

Now why would that be?

August 2005

SPEAKING FROM THE HEART

You might be interested in a few quotes from various EU officials and other like-minded characters, though I recommend the application of two fingers of scotch before you continue, and go easy on the ice: "The Europe of Maastricht could only have been created in the absence of democracy": (Claude Cheysson, ex-French Foreign Minister and member of the EU Commission)...

"I have never understood why public opinion about European issues should be taken into account": (Raymond Barre, ex-French Prime Minister and Commissioner)...

"I look forward to the day when the Westminster Parliament is just a council chamber in Europe": (Kenneth Clark, whilst Chancellor of the Exchequer in 1996 – International Currency Review, Vol 23, No 4, if you're interested)...

"Neither the Constitutional text nor the ideas contained in it are dead. There's no doubt that sooner or later the EU will have a foreign minister and a diplomatic service": Javier Solana, the EU Commission's high representative, and the man who already has his knees under the desk marked EU Foreign Minister.

I should finish by pointing out that Brussels is busy establishing EU Embassies all over the world, whilst at the same time Britain is busily closing hers down. Of the last nine we have recently shut, seven were in Commonwealth countries. Draw your own conclusions.

August 2005

THE DARWIN AWARDS

I once had a neighbour who enjoyed going out for a drink most evenings, usually returning after midnight, parking with the aid of his dustbins. This was deep in the Dorset countryside and he got away with it for a while until the Police caught up with him, after which he would catch me on the way to work and bemoan the lack of a rural bus service. As far as I was concerned, he'd made his bed and should now make himself comfortable.

The 2005 Darwin Awards are a case in point. When robber James Elliot fired a .38 revolver at his victim in Long Beach, California, the gun wouldn't fire, so he peered down the barrel and tried the trigger again. This time it fired.

Another one to catch my eye was a female shopper in New York whose purse was snatched. She gave the cops a description of the thief and they quickly arrested a suspect and drove him back to the shop for a positive ID. The thief got out of the squad car and said: "Yes officer, that's her. That's the lady I stole the purse from."

My own favourite is from Zimbabwe, when a bus driver transporting 20 mental patients from Harare to Bulawayo pulled off the road and had a few drinks at a bar en-route. By the time he returned to the bus, the passengers had all escaped. The driver went to a nearby bus stop and offered everyone a free ride. He then delivered them to the mental asylum, explaining to the staff that his passengers were "excitable and prone to bizarre fantasies". It took three days before the deception was discovered...

None of which has anything to do with the European Union, but at least proves that Brussels doesn't have a total monopoly on stupid behaviour.

August 2005

HOW MUCH?

If British voters had ever realised the true cost of Britain's membership of the European Union they would have been running away from Brussels like a chicken with the Colonel after it. Let's look at a few of those costs.

Our 2005/2006 gross contribution to the EU will be £39-million a day (or £14.238 billion annually)...How many hospitals or schools would that fund?... True, we get some of the money back, but with strings. Any project must be acceptable to Brussels, must advertise the EU's involvement (with a logo of the blue flag, and gold stars) and must usually be match-funded by our own government.

This is the equivalent of you giving me £10, and me giving you £5 in return, insisting that before you spend it, you'll have to ask my permission, and stump up another fiver from your own pocket (match-funding).

Further costs of EU membership are all those rules, directives and regulations, and the cost of implementing them (by civil servants) and of complying with them (industry, business, and ultimately the tax-payer). It depends who you ask but the total COST SAVINGS of withdrawal from the EU are jaw-dropping.

The British Chamber of Commerce recently estimated that EU regulations cost the UK economy £37.5 billion per annum, and Ian Milne's scholarly study - relying totally on officially released figures – concludes that the most likely total is £40-billion.

This is comprised of the £5-billion net contribution, £15-billion for the Common Agricultural Policy, and £20-billion for the cost of EU regulations. In the absence of official government figures (despite constant requests from all quarters) the Ian Milne sums are probably the best bet.

So the next time somebody praises all those wonderful projects funded by Brussels, you should have the necessary ammunition to bring them down to earth.

August 2005

"NON"

When the French and Dutch voted "No" to the EU Constitution commentators asked how it could have happened. French voters had felt that the Constitution was too "Anglo Saxon", whilst the Dutch were worried that the social experiment of multiculturalism and immigration (enforced by political correctness and positive discrimination) was swamping traditional Dutch culture.

In Britain, had we been asked to vote, our reasons for saying "No" would have been different again.

The common thread running through all of this is a distrust of officialdom and remote governments. But the EU leaders cannot see this. Mr Barrosso, in Brussels, says that the "No" results show that the people want "more Europe". Not only is this contrary to common sense, it is the reasoning of the madhouse, because the real nature of the EU is a top-down conglomeration of different nations and cultures, all squeezed together into a naïve and idealistic stew.

Far from being the solution, the EU has become the problem, with the underlying tensions and strains now in evidence. But they were always apparent from the beginning... A trading arrangement with cross border agreements on various matters such as ease of travel, pollution standards or criminal extradition, would worry no-one and make good sense.

But it has morphed into a vast Frankenstein's monster, in which British soldiers, for example, are now going into action with the EU symbol on their cap badge, and will soon be required to swear allegiance not to Her Majesty the Queen but to the European Union itself...Whatever else you may feel, it sure isn't just a Common Market anymore.

September 2005

SHAKINGS FROM THE TREE

UKIP has a useful researcher named Steve Reed who has recently sent me a few pieces of information which might be of interest.

POSTAL SERVICES: the EU directives 96/67/EC and 2002/39/EC made it illegal for Royal Mail to subsidise unprofitable parts or to have exclusive rights to carry certain weights of mail. This resulted in contractors (some of them subsidised) cherry-picking the best delivery routes and beggaring the Service, leading to closure of post offices, rising charges, and falling standards (aggravated by casual agency staff replacing career postal workers).

RAIL SERVICE: the EU directives 91/440/EEC, 96/48/EC, and 2004/49/EC all conspired to wreck our train system. In the same story as the Post Office, it was made illegal for British Rail to own its own track (cue Railtrack and the ensuing saga of Stephen Byers etc), whilst opening up freight and passenger contracts meant that standards inevitably slipped as rivals snapped up the profitable parts, leaving a decayed and redundant shell.

I D CARDS: EU directives 2002/334/EC and 2002/1030/EC introduced requirements for biometric data in identity documents for EU residents from countries outside the EU...But the meat of this particular pie comes in an EU Commission statement from early in 2005. I quote: " Another proposal for the inclusion of biometrics and personal data in relation to the documents of EU citizens will follow later this year".

The above examples hopefully show you that when the British Government announces a certain policy, the real reason often has nothing to do with common sense or good governance, but is because the European Union has demanded it. A further example is VAT. Before we joined the Common Market this tax was unknown in Britain. But once we had joined, we became liable, reaching deeper into our pockets yet again.... all to pursue the naïve chimera of a common European identity which has never existed and probably never will.

September 2005

'AIR THICK WITH FEATHERS' SHOCK

Next time you are in the North-East Region of England, listen very carefully and you might hear the sort of squawking and commotion usually associated with a hen coop when the farmer has toddled off to bed, leaving the gate wide open.

Allow me to explain. Without asking the public Britain has been divided up into twelve Euro regions, but up in the North-East Region Tony Blair decided to hold a referendum to make everything nice and official. That was in November 2004, and the voters replied to him with a trumpeting raspberry, a resounding "No" to an elected assembly, so they were stuck with an unelected one, like everybody else.

In July 2005 the North East Assembly members announced they were setting themselves up as a limited company.... The reason was Neil Herron, a staunch opponent of regional assemblies (and one of the leaders of the Metric Martyr campaign) who had publicised the awkward fact that the individual members of the Assembly were "personally responsible for all its financial obligations, including the contracts and pension rights of its employees. Between them they had thus unwittingly taken on liabilities amounting to millions of pounds" (Christopher Booker, Sunday Times July 2005).

The North-East Assembly then tried to set up their limited company, only to find that Mr Herron had got there first, registering that name for himself. Rubbing caustic into the wound Herron then pointed out that under the 1985 Companies Act setting up such a limited company still would not absolve members from individual liabilities. But his next shot hit them below the waterline.

Some Assembly members were also serving councillors, but by voting for their councils to grant money to the Assembly (money paid by council tax payers) they were in breach of the 1972 Local Government Act which forbids councillors to give public money to any project in which they have a personal financial stake.

The Police have been informed and, at the time of writing, are investigating.

September 2005

Regional Assemblies are now being closed down. The Government is trying a new tactic of unitary authorities. Same bloke. Different hat.

AH...FARMER GILES.
I'VE BEEN EXPECTING YOU

It would be nice to think that despite every sign to the contrary, the Labour Government cared about Britain's farming industry. But even that faint hope looks increasingly fragile. Private Eye magazine refers to Margaret Beckett, head of Defra, as 'Rosa Kleb', and the following explains why. Firstly, Rosa Kleb is the wicked SMERSH agent in 007's 'From Russia With Love', operating mostly from behind a desk in Moscow.

Nick Somerfield, a senior member of the Farming Union of Wales, made an appointment to see Mrs Beckett in her London office just off Millbank. He was shown into the room by a hushed official. "Rosa" was seated at the desk, studying paperwork, and did not acknowledge his presence. Mr Somerfield waited for a while. Still Rosa did not raise her gaze. Mr Somerfield cleared his throat. Still she did not look up...

Mr Somerfield broke the silence, explaining that he wanted to make sure she understood the views of Welsh farmers. To quote Private Eye magazine (8/7/05): "Without raising her eyes Rosa icily observed that if she wanted to know the views of farmers she would ask her officials at Defra. After a shocked pause, realising that the interview for which he had travelled 200 miles up to London was at an end. Somerfield left the room and set off back to Wales."

So there you have it. The new battle cry of SMERSH. "Death to Farmers."

September 2005

EUROPE OR BUST

We joined the EU (then the Common Market) in the 1970's. At the time, many Britons thought that it was probably a good idea. But like a cyclist going through a car-wash, we got more than we bargained for.

One problem, of course, is that we didn't bargain; we didn't even make an attempt at bargaining. Edward Heath was so relieved to get in that he rolled over doggy-fashion, giving up our fishing grounds without even demanding access to the Mediterranean for our own fleet. With friends like that, who needs enemies? In terms of Shakespearean criticism, Mr Heath played the king as if someone had just played the ace.

And when a politician damages the interests of their own people, the people whom they've been elected to serve, in my book that goes beyond incompetence. Some observers have seen this as treachery, a betrayal of the nation, to be condemned and despised; but in the end the judgement on Mr Heath is probably a matter of personal opinion and the passage of time. History will decide.

One example of the antics that went on: the European Movement, with the blessing of Heath, set about changing public attitudes to joining the Common Market (At the time, 70% were opposed to membership). They met secretly at the Connaught Hotel in London: MP's, industrialists, Managing Director of BBC Radio Ian Trethowan, and a shadowy organisation called IRD, a dirty tricks dept of the Foreign Office. Also present was Nigel Ryan, Editor of ITN.

This group, funded in part by the tax-payer, set about a campaign of psychological warfare on the sub-conscious of the nation, including letters to newspapers, written by the IRD, signed every Wednesday by the MPs, inserting a letter into the Times almost daily for two years. The Today programme was targeted, along with World at One, Women's Hour, and Panorama. They even handed out free newspapers, using nubile girls in T-shirts (the slogan was "Europe or Bust".)

But then they hit a problem. One of the presenters of the Today programme, Jack de Manio, was a euro realist, and he baulked at what was going on. And so the BBC got rid of him. Roy Hattersley, MP, claims to have been so disturbed by this that he refused to attend another meeting, though his concern did not extend to telling the British People what was going on behind their backs.

Any sceptics among you can refer to Radio 4's: "Document: A letter to the Times", broadcast on 3/2/2000, presented by Christopher Cook. It's all there, including interviews with Sir Edward Heath and with Lord Hattersley, who at least has the grace to admit: "Joining the European Community did involve significant loss of sovereignty but by telling the British people that was not involved I think the rest of the argument was prejudiced for the next 20, 30 years". How right he is.

Does such Government-manipulation remind anyone of the present debate over the euro? History repeating itself; the first time as tragedy, the second time as farce?

September 2005

SOME SUPERSTATE

If you accuse the EU of becoming a centralised Superstate, you will sometimes be greeted with a sort of complacent chortle from those who disagree. "Don't be so absurd. The EU employs fewer people than Leeds City Council, for heaven's sake. Some Superstate!"

I'm afraid this is a blind alley. At the end of Queen Victoria's reign the British Raj ruled 300-million Indians, using barely 1,500 British administrators in the Indian Civil Service and 3,000 or so British officers in the Indian Army, with probably fewer than 20,000 Britons running the entire country, fewer than the officials directly employed in Brussels.

But the main point is that Brussels churns out an avalanche of rules and regulations across Europe to be implemented by national civil servants and agencies. The Commission is the humming dynamo at the centre, but its 40,000 or so officials are merely the tip of the iceberg, a nexus linking hundreds of thousands of employees across Europe, all of them implementing rules from the EU to be imposed in a country near you.

And what is more, there's not a single thing you can do about it, because unlike Leed's City Council, you cannot vote out the EU.

October 2005

UP THE CREEK,
WITH NO MEANS OF PROPULSION

It makes you wonder whose side they're on...In August 2005 the Scottish Executive awarded a contract to build a fisheries protection vessel. But despite Scotland's long history of shipbuilding the contract went not to the Ferguson yard in Port Glasgow but to a Polish yard in Gdansk, Remontowa, which at the time stood accused of receiving illegal subsidies from the Polish Government.

The Scottish Executive held up its hands and effectively said: "Don't blame us, blame the EU and its procurement rules. We were prevented from giving preferential treatment to a Scottish yard."

The Scottish MPs were steaming with anger and no-one can blame them: Trish Goodman, Labour for West Renfrewshire, said she was deeply angry and bitterly disappointed at the weak-kneed betrayal of the Ferguson workforce, and senior ministers should be ashamed of themselves: "The Scottish Executive and its officials have cut these men and women adrift in their overcautious and spineless approach to the EU and its rules."

The SNP's deputy director, Nicola Sturgeon, went even further: "It's an absolute disgrace that a Scottish company now faces closure. This tendering process has been a shambles from the start and now the workers at Ferguson and their families will suffer as a direct result of the First Minister's failure to protect Scottish interests. It is a betrayal. Scotland and Scottish shipbuilding deserve better than this" (The Scotsman 5/8/05).

It has recently been revealed that a contract to build a ferry for Caledonian MacBrayne also went to the Polish yard – still under investigation at the time – because it offered "best value."

To those of us familiar with the workings of the EU none of the above will sound at all surprising. What lifts an eyebrow is the fact that Scottish politicians have taken so long to cotton on to the Byzantine nature of the Brussels madhouse.

October 2005

STAMPING THEIR LITTLE FEET

UKIP has recently launched a nationwide newspaper campaign for Britain to leave the EU, called "Let the People Decide". At first glance a newspaper editor might think this attention-grabber about as useful as an ashtray on a motorbike, or as earth-shattering as the infamous headline "Man, 87, Dies"... But UKIP's campaign has caused a marvellous storm in the political world because we are using EU funds to pay for it; and the Labour Party is squealing in protest (which is always nice to see).

Labour MEP Stephen Hughes fulminated: "This is a disgraceful abuse of parliamentary funds. It's wrong that money meant for promoting the work of the institution is being used to undermine it." Almost stamping his foot in tearful frustration, he went on: "They are using the money to undermine everything we work for!"

To which UKIP effectively replied: "Yep, that's right, Chum, that's exactly what we're doing."

Gary Titley (another Labour MEP) took up the call: "This fund was originally intended for the dissemination of information, rather than political campaigning."

UKIP was unrepentant. Nigel Farage, their parliamentary leader in Brussels, explained: "It is a perfectly valid use of the money. We are delighted with the irony of the situation. I did not hear complaints from Mr Titley when his own group spent their information budget interfering in the referendums in Ireland, Denmark, France, Holland and Malta. All we are doing is a little to redress the balance."

Mr Farage was right. The EU recently spent its entire information budget promoting the now-failed Constitution and not one cent upon the arguments against. And millions of euros are lavished upon promoting European integration by supporting federalist think-tanks, seminars, the Charlemagne Prize, and information campaigns in schools and colleges to brainwash the children – with books such as: "Europe, My Country" - not to mention a vast network of university professorships and the like.

UKIP's campaign "LET THE PEOPLE DECIDE", a vote on getting out of the EU, will be coming to you soon. Please respond and send a huge message that Britain has had enough of the EU, and wants out.

October 2005

AS FAIR AS THE BLACK DEATH

Commenting on the Poll Tax in 1989 the Tory Reform Group predicted: "It has all the makings of a disaster. The poll tax is fair only in the sense that the Black Death was fair".... And they were right: it was a complete dog's dinner, costing £12 per-head to collect, compared to the old rates at £5. When the tax was introduced it was followed by riots in London and a revolt in the Tory shires. In West Oxfordshire eighteen Tory councillors resigned en-bloc and when their leader stood for re-election as an independent he beat the Conservative by a factor of four!

One example may prove how the people of Britain were conned. Back in 1990 the Government estimated that the then-new Poll Tax in Dover and Chelmsford would be respectively £150 and £181. The actual bills were £298 and £397. The public had been shafted.

Then the Government loaded extra responsibilities onto councils while suppressing Income Tax. They still got their money, but the councils did the dirty work. Since then our present councils have heaped on the misery, advertising non-jobs such as Racial Diversity Officers, Children's Play Co-ordinators, Corporate Social Inclusion Managers (at a cool £55,000 a year) and the recent classic 'Decriminalisation of Parking Enforcement Project Implementation Manager'.

Far from cutting back on their bloated public services New Labour (soon to become Newish Old Labour) have taken on 100,000 extra staff in the last year alone. And are most of these new recruits the people we really need? the doctors, nurses, teachers or policemen who act as the social glue holding this country together?

You really don't need me to answer that, do you?

November 2005

ABOUT AS SATISFYING AS TRIPPING A DWARF

Soon after we regained the ashes last September, Dr Injat Singh appeared on Radio 4's "Thought For the Day". He began with these words: "Cricket is full of politically-incorrect terms like 'short leg' and 'silly mid off'."

Perhaps I'm missing something here, but if Dr Singh is correct and 'short leg' is now politically incorrect then this country has lost the plot. More worryingly, no-one at Radio 4 picked him up on it.

Political correctness started life as a well-meaning attempt at preventing idiots from giving unnecessary offence to others, but it has mutated into an out of control monster of cultural Marxism. PC is social engineering through mind control; you are told what to think, how to think, and when to think it.

Those in the BBC or in Government Service wanting to build a career, have to nod, smile encouragingly, and pretend to go along with it. If they complain, their future job might involve asking the next person in the queue whether they want fries with that.

In the early 1980s certain professionals in the NHS decided to shut down virtually all of the old mental handicap and psychiatric hospitals, shunting the patients out into "the Community" under a process called "normalisation".

These professionals probably meant well, but the net result was that the old asylums closed down, leaving nowhere for those who needed the genuine *asylum* of sheltered living away from this rough real world...As for the patients – cosily renamed 'clients' – most were dumped into grotty bedsits; pretty much alone, isolated, and missing the stimulus of the human company of staff and the other patients. Thousands of these displaced people inevitably found themselves in prison because life in the outside world became too difficult to handle, a fact usually glossed over by those responsible for the whole fiasco.

Political correctness smothered dissent and allowed this to happen, and now stands in the dock. When failure becomes "deferred success", when accident blackspots become "hotspots", when school sports days are banned because not every child can win, and when prison officers are banned from wearing a cancer charity badge depicting the Cross of St George because it might be considered racist, what more proof is needed that PC is thriving, and must be fought at every crossroads and every bend in the road.

November 2005

SIGNS OF THE TIMES

There are signs, and then there are signs. For example, beside a motorway in Ireland: "If You Can Read This Sign, You're Travelling in the Wrong Direction", or on a packet of candles: "Warning - Hot When Lit". I also rather liked the sign: "No Wasps" which is pretty surreal if you think about it for a moment.

But the other type of signs are entertaining because they unintentionally reveal secrets, like Ken Clarke pretending that Europe is a non-issue for the Tories.

The best signs of all came at the recent Lib-Dem Party Conference, when the grassroots membership threw out a proposal to limit the spending of the European Parliament... Leading modernisers reacted with fury: Dr Vincent Cable, their Treasury Spokesman, could hardly contain himself, branding the entire group of Lib-Dem MEPs: 'the ostrich tendency'. He appealed to the delegates almost with tears in his eyes: "We will not win the argument with a sceptical British public without reform" (of the way Brussels spends our cash).

Sarah Teather, Local Government spokeswoman, then condemned the eurofanatics as "self indulgent and irresponsible" just when the Party needed to emphasise its credibility. She went on: "Given the deficit in the European Union's finances, giving it a blank cheque is no way to demonstrate responsibility, no way to demonstrate reform."

But the Lib Dems' grassroots couldn't care less about EU reform. Their mainly Socialist activists are very happy with the status quo and want us in deeper; their MEP's are even on record as saying: "We must pay up. We can't have Europe on the cheap."

On the 'Europe' issue the Lib Dems are trying to stare out the people. They were punished for this in 2004 when UKIP pushed them into 4th place in the European elections, and the same will happen again.

Even someone with the brains of a TV weathergirl could read the signs that you don't win elections by telling the voters that they are wrong, particularly when they are right.

November 2005

ROWLOCKS, WE WON

Last year Lord Sebastian Coe unveiled the London bid for the Olympics. He was inspired by the late-President Kennedy, using these words: "We shouldn't ask what these Olympic Games can do for us, we should ask what they can do for our children".... Well I can tell Lord Coe what the Games will probably do for our children. It will saddle them with a mountain of debt that will take years to clear. There are people in Montreal, not born when the Olympic Games took place, still paying for it in their taxes.

The UK Independence Party is campaigning for the Games to go to Paris, Why should Londoners (and the rest of us) be landed with the cost of this event?

The Greek Finance Minister, Giorgos Alogoskoufis, recently admitted that the cost of the Athens Games was £6.31-billion, not including the expenses on infrastructure.

The supposed boost to employment never happened. Within a week of the athletes' departure, thousands of Greek construction and service-industry personnel were thrown out of work, many of them unpaid. Like all such grandiose schemes the bid for the London Games is based on soaring egotism, rather than on a proper plan for urban regeneration.

The silver lining to this is that both Ken Livingstone and Cherie Blair are publicly backing the London Games, which should ensure that they go to Paris.

November 2005

You can't win them all. And we certainly lost this one.

BEYOND BELIEF

The future leadership of the Tory Party is none of my business, but of the two contenders, at the time of writing, David Cameron seems to be the bookies favourite among ordinary Tory members

An article in The Times (19.10.05) by Andrew Pierce addressed Mr Cameron's stance on matters EU and concluded that it was deeply suspect. Only six weeks after Black Wednesday when Britain was bundled out of the Exchange Rate Mechanism, Mr Cameron (then an advisor to Chancellor Norman Lamont) was arguing that there were still benefits to dumping the pound and joining the euro.

To quote the newspaper: "In the memo, a copy of which has been passed to The Times, Mr Cameron said: 'There is no doubt that a single currency would have a number of benefits. Transaction costs and exchange-rate risks would be eliminated and, as a result, trade would increase substantially. Also, a central bank and a single currency, if established in the right way, could help to make Europe a zone of permanently low inflation."

So whilst Norman Lamont was singing in his bath, and most Tories were relieved to be out of the ERM, allowing Britain to finally climb out of recession, Mr Cameron had apparently already dismissed other options such as not joining the euro. This seems odd, from someone who now describes himself as Eurosceptic and wishes to reclaim powers back from Brussels.

November 2005

NO2ID

Some of you may feel that ID cards are a good idea if they prevent terrorism, illegal immigration or organised crime, but please consider the following. The Government has already admitted the minimum cost will be £5.6 Billion (or six domes!) and that figure will inevitably spiral upwards, not including the charges for the ID cards, penalties for errors that you might make, and the cost of policing the scheme. Also, the cards will inevitably be faked. If man made it, then man can fake it.

The Government is also creating a new Identity Agency, which is good news for the Civil Service but not for the beleaguered taxpayer.

May I quote from a recent leaflet from the NO.2.ID group: "You are about to be fingerprinted, eye-scanned and tagged like a criminal. Any errors will be your responsibility...about 100 people a month (out of a few thousand checked) are wrongly marked as criminals by the Criminal Records Bureau...What happens to your life when the scanner fails or there's a mistake?"

Worst danger of all is the National Identity Register, a database on us all, which will have to be compulsory, containing details on your purchasing history, your finances, political leanings, religion, possibly even your physical whereabouts or your DNA.

The State governs with our permission, deriving its power by common consent of the people. Under a dictatorship things would be less cosy, but we are a democracy, and there lies the difference. But even if you trust this government to act responsibly, what about one in 20-year's time?

As for crime prevention, the ID cards will do very little.

No mugger or burglar will carry one, nor will it prevent home-grown terrorists from wearing a Semtex girdle. The icing on the cake is that ID cards are being steadily introduced across the entire European Union, for ease of monitoring of all "citizens". Do you really want to be told by Brussels to carry a card or be fined?

As the NO.2.ID people say: "The ID scheme is expensive and socially destructive. Either it will help make Britain a police state, or it will be a bigger white elephant than the poll tax."

UKIP is totally opposed to compulsory ID cards and to the National Identity Register, which will enable the government to view you under a microscope. For more information on this you could try

www.NO2ID.net

December 2005

INTO THE DEEP END

FRES is the highly secret Future Rapid Effect System, the British Army's new generation of satellite-coordinated weapons and vehicles, intended to link us up with the 66,000-strong EU Rapid Reaction Force - which is the main reason why Britain recently abolished or merged 19 historic regiments such as the Black Watch - little to do with efficiency or making savings.

FRES needs a European satellite such as Galileo in order to work, and is incompatible with America's GPS system, making it impossible for FRES-equipped units to operate alongside US forces (eg: the European system would identify US units as the enemy, which is probably how Chirac feels towards the Yanks but no matter).

We are being sucked into the new EU Army at a breathtaking rate, with massive contracts going to European firms in preference to bids from joint US-UK consortia. One example is the new replacement for Land Rovers. The MoD has awarded the contract for the new Panther vehicle to Italian firm Iveco at £413,000 each, four times the cost of a Humvee.

Even more puzzling is the £1.6-billion contract which recently went to Man-Nutzfahrzeuge trucks in Germany, when two US-British consortia had offered better vehicles to be built here in Britain by British workers. But thanks to EU rules, preference must be given to wholly European firms.

Another example is the Storm Shadow, a French cruise missile which we have bought for a cool £1-million each. Had we bought the longer-range and lighter JASSM missile, built by US Lockheed Martin, we could have got them for only £167,000 apiece. But if you're American or even in partnership with them, then forget it...

Going back to those trucks bought from Germany. Man Nutzfahrzeuge also produces an electronic fleet-management system called TELEMATICS, already compatible with the EU's "Network Centre Logistics" military programme. Having bought the trucks we will probably end up buying TELEMATICS as well, which in turn will mean purchasing a new European electronic combat system, because combat and logistics need to link together.

As we wade further and deeper into the pool we will soon find ourselves out beyond our depth. The

Americans are not perfect, but they have been good friends and allies to us over the last hundred years. And looking at the alternative, a squabbling, bickering, backbiting EU that doesn't even speak the same language, personally I would rather depend on the Americans any day of the week.

December 2005

With thanks to Dr Richard North

2006

LE 'ALF INCH

Give 'em an inch and they'll take 1.609km...and the pint, the acre, and the rest of them. Under John Major in 1994, we promised Brussels to dump imperial measurements in favour of metric. True, we retain an opt-out clause (a 'derogation' in Euro-babble) to commit cultural suicide in our own time, rather like leaving a loaded pistol on the table for us. But at some point we have to do it. And Brussels is getting impatient.

Gunter Verheugen, EU commissioner on enterprise and industry, recently told the UK government to fix a date "as soon as possible" for scrapping imperial: "They are running behind on this. In legal terms it is clear they have committed themselves to the metric system. Now we have to see how to deal with it"...And if we fail to comply we could then be taken to the European court in Strasbourg, which would force us, because EU law beats our own every time, as the late-Steve Thoburn proved with the Metric Martyrs' case and the most famous bunch of bananas in history.

Many road signs currently reading "100-Yards Ahead" have actually been sited 100-metres from the junction because when the changeover occurs it will be easier to swop the sign than move the pole...Last to disappear will be the pint of beer because once that has gone the EU's victory will be obvious to the British working man. Until then the EU will continue in its own underhand and sneaky way, aided and abetted by those within the walls.

Even the BBC are involved in this metric brainwashing. During the first Gulf War, BBC reporter John Simpson was doing a piece to camera: "The enemy positions are located 5 kilometres down the valley." At this point his words were drowned by a screaming whooshing sound overhead. Everybody dropped flat and the air filled with smoke, dust, and falling rocks. A moment later Simpson's voice could be heard: "Bloody hell...that was twenty feet away!"

Whilst on holiday in Normandy an acquaintance of mine went into a French garage looking for a length of copper pipe: "I need a piece of 12.5mm, please". Puzzlement, then, **"Ah Monsieur, le 'alf inch"**. Apparently bicycle wheels in France are also sized in imperial, along with most plumbing fittings. And while we're on the subject, if the metric system is so superior why do the French persist in packing their champagne in cases of twelve?

The serious aspect to this is not merely the astronomical cost of converting all those car speedometers, roadsigns, pint glasses, etc... Most damaging is the cultural implications.

A country is more than just a set of measurements, but if you deliberately set about dismantling the pillars upon which it is based (including its historical measuring system) then eventually all that remains is a useless pile of rubble.

January 2006

HELLO MR PLOD

There are two basic reactions to the British police. If a patrol car appears in the rear-view mirror when we're driving along, most of us suffer a moment's guilty unease: Was I speeding? Is the tax or MOT out? When did I last check the tyres? In effect, a respect for the rules that hold society together.

The alternative reaction to the law is to give that patrol car the finger out of the window.

Given the importance of how we view the police (and the justice system in general) it is vital that they keep our support. But thanks to political correctness, they seem intent on losing it. When Mary Magilton was struck by a hit-and-run vehicle last October, she described the offending driver as "fat". The WPC from Greater Manchester Police gave her a frosty look and ticked her off for using 'inappropriate language'. Mrs Magilton said: "The police reaction was dismissive and apathetic. They didn't even get me to sign a statement. They treated me with such disdain. I don't know any other words to describe a fat person. People describe me as skinny with fuzzy hair and it doesn't bother me."

Or take the case of Amerjit Singh, a 26-year old police constable, one of the first Sikhs to be recruited by Cambridgeshire Constabulary and exactly the sort of person we need to recruit in a multi-racial Britain... PC Singh received an official verbal warning for using "too much force" restraining a suicidal man - high on drink and drugs - from leaping out of a second-floor window. PC Singh's MP, Stewart Jackson (Tory) described this reprimand as "barking mad" and one has to agree.

Of course we must remember that we now live in a country where a teenaged girl in Worcester recently persuaded a court not to electronically tag her because she preferred skirts and disliked wearing trousers (the poor lamb). Her own MP, Michael Foster (Labour) said: "These magistrates seem to be taking the mickey. Sometimes I pull my hair out at these decisions."

If you can work it out, please drop me a line at Trago Mills. But I won't be hovering around that letterbox.

January 2006

THE THORN BEHIND THE ROSE

Tony Blair came back from the Brussels-Budget summit in December, having surrendered £7-billion of our money to the EU. As a negotiator he was dismal: outsmarted and outmanoeuvred by the French. The Foreign Minister, Phillipe Douste-Blazy said: "Jacques Chirac has secured that there won't be reform of the Common Agricultural Policy before 2014", and asked how the French Government would respond to a review in 2009 another official said: "We would veto it"

So... game, set and match to Paris. But at least they were looking after their own people.

Blair's claimed 'victory' was that giving states such as Poland or Hungary a bundle of cash would improve their ailing economies and turn them into better trading partners for us. Result: everybody wins. But the thorn behind the rose is that this is bunkum.

Here are the 2004 trade figures comparing UK and German exports to these countries in millions of pounds: UK to Poland £1409 (Germany £12,711), UK to Hungary £971 (Germany £8675), and UK to Czech Republic £930 (Germany £12,020). Who exactly will benefit most from economic expansion in the East? According to the Financial Times (19/12/05) there is a further twist to this, which may explain why Gordon Brown was even grumpier than usual. The British rebate will remain untouched until 2009, but whoever wins the general election in that year will have to find the extra £7-billion between then and 2013... a nice present for Gordon Brown when he re-enters No 10.

January 2006

Tony Blair stepped down early, just failing to beat Margaret Thatcher's record 10-year term in office. At the time of writing (Spring 2008) things seem less rosy for Gordon Brown, but whoever ultimately wins the election, they will still face this invoice from the EU. As usual, the British taxpayer will be paying.

IN THE DAZ, IN THE WATER...

I recently had the misfortune of attending a training exercise for a large organisation, which started badly and then got worse. As a warm-up we were asked to name one item from the Twentieth Century that had most changed our lives. And without exception - without exception – everyone chose the mobile phone. I knew I was in trouble when I suggested the automatic washing machine and got a blank look in return. [I was used to it by then...if you want me, just look for the only man in the bus queue facing the wrong way).

Having established myself as odd one out, and almost at the speed of 'greased lightning, oh greased lightning' - faster indeed than John Prescott with a Big-Mac voucher - we moved on to Appropriate Terms in the Workplace, where we learnt that Workmen are now 'Workers', Manning the phones is now 'Staffing the phones', Deaf and Dumb is 'Deaf Without Speech' and brain-storming sessions have morphed into 'Thought Showers' (The last I'd heard they were Cloud-Bursting but that's obviously old hat).

The delegates also learnt that henceforth they would not be working in teams but in 'Clusters', and also that it was vital to avoid 'Silo Thinking', and on this I totally agree. Silos not only contain chicken-feed but also missiles, and it is important that one doesn't explode in an 'inappropriate' location. But if anybody's interested, I can supply a highly 'appropriate' map reference.

February 2006

PORRIDGE FOR ALL

From January 1st 2006 every offence in Britain has become "arrestable". Motoring infringements, dropping litter, wearing a loud tie in a residential area after midnight; all of them could see you banged up in a police cell. We can thank disgraced ex-Home Secretary David Blunkett for this, and his Serious Organised Crime and Police Act which was sneaked through Parliament with barely a whisper from the MP's. And as time goes on, this will profoundly alter the relationship between the police and the general public.

The police claim there are safeguards in place to prevent abuses, but an officer may carry out an arrest to allow the prompt and "effective investigation of the offence or of the conduct of the person in question", and also "to prevent any prosecution of the offence from being hindered by the disappearance of the person in question". This is effectively a blank cheque to any officer if they don't like the look of you. The KGB could have operated very well under that sort of restriction.

Even more sinister is that the police are now empowered, using force if necessary, to take DNA samples, fingerprints and mug-shots for all but the most minor of offences. Bear in mind that at this point you have not been convicted of anything, and under British law are innocent until proven guilty.

Quoting journalist Henry Porter (The Observer 6/11/05): "Most solicitors who deal with the police on a daily basis are convinced that these new powers criminalize the public". He goes on: "Arresting someone, photographing and forcibly taking samples from them places an individual in an entirely different relationship with the state from the one most of us have known... MP's of all hues now have a grave responsibility. They are the stewards of our democracy and they should damn well start behaving like it."

February 2006

AS CLOSE TO A FOOT

The Palace of Westminster produces a ruler as a memento for visitors. One side of the ruler is blank. The other side is measured in centimetres and millimetres, up to 30cm, identical along both edges, for that is all metric can offer.

When asked how 30cm is divisible into one metre, the Palace official replied: "Er, well actually it isn't". And when asked: "So why 30cm then?" he responded: "It's as close as we could get to a foot."

How ironic that this lifeless metric system should be a relic of the French Revolution, the Reign of Terror, when the monarchy and church were overthrown along with the nation's former culture. The revolutionaries also imposed a decimal clock and calendar, which lasted only a year or two because they simply didn't work.

Vivian Linacre, President of the British Weights and Measures Association, wrote to the EU in 1998, asking about compulsory metrication for Britain. The then-EU Commissioner for Industry, Martin Bangemann, got back to him: "Mr Linacre, you have to understand, Britain is in an anomalous position, being a full partner in the EU, yet using a common system of weights and measures with the USA, thereby gaining an unfair advantage in transatlantic trade."

On January 1st 2010 Britain must give up its remaining Imperial measurements, by order of the EU because our "derogation" then expires. It may be extended if there is a public outcry, but the threat remains and is rooted in the EU's visceral loathing for America and her cultural bond with us. Our language has been enriched by these words: inch, foot, furlong, mile, fathom, acre, ounce, stone, pint, quart, gallon. As Mr Linacre says: " the names are integral to the English language. They are beautiful as well as practical. The Bible and Shakespeare are full of them".

If you care about this destruction of our traditional measurements, or merely want some information, please contact Vivian Linacre at *vtlinacre@yahoo.co.uk*, or at 21 Marshall Place, Perth, PH2 8AG…. As he says, we could have only four more years before the total imposition of metric.

February 2006

With gratitude to V. Linacre for the use of his November 2005 article.

A YAWNING GAP

The euro currency has become a huge yawn in Britain because there is no possibility that we will dump sterling for many years. But things get more interesting when we look at Italy.

According to Charles Dumas of the highly respected economic think-tank Lombard Street Research: "Italian labour costs are beyond the point of being compatible with EMU membership without painful reforms. The budget deficit is being widened to make up for loss of export market share. Public debt is heading up towards 150% of GDP. The political mess in Rome means exit from EMU is virtually inevitable."

HSBC, the world's second largest bank, warned that some countries might actually benefit from ditching the euro. In their 2005 paper European Meltdown? they deemed Italy the prime candidate for exit (higher even than Germany and Holland) because it was trapped in slump with a "truly appalling export performance", and Rome might benefit from switching its existing national debt from euros to a weaker "new lira".

As HSBC said: "The thing about sovereign debt is that the sovereign can do just about anything it likes on domestic debt because it enacts the law that governs those securities."

The real weakness of the euro is that it runs on the principle of 'one size fits all', which cannot work, any more than assuming that one pair of trousers will fit everyone in the room. I know it, you know it, the British people know it; HSBC knows it. But as usual Brussels is completely clueless.

February 2006 (continued on next page)

With hindsight that first sentence proves untrue. Article 3 of the new Treaty says: "The Union shall establish an economic and monetary union whose currency is the euro." And goes on to desire: "ever closer co-ordination of economic policies… pending the euro becoming the currency of all Member States of the Union." No excuse for yawning, after all.

DON'T LIKE IT? THERE'S THE DOOR

This is a cut-down version of a recent article apparently from a national newspaper and I felt that you might be interested. The headline was 'Immigrants Not Brits Must Adapt'.

"I am tired of this nation worrying about whether we are offending some individual or their culture. Since the July 7th terrorist attacks we have experienced a surge in patriotism by the majority of Brits. However, the disgust about the attacks had barely settled when the politically correct crowd began complaining about the possibility that our patriotism was offending others.

'I am not against immigration, nor do I hold a grudge against anyone seeking a better life coming to Britain. Our population is made up of descendants of immigrants. However there are a few things that those recently arrived in our country, and apparently some born here, need to understand. This idea of multiculturalism has served only to dilute our sovereignty and our national identity. We have our own culture, society, language and lifestyle, developed over centuries by millions of men and women who have sought freedom.

'We speak ENGLISH, not Indian, Urdu, Arabic, Chinese or any other language. Therefore if you wish to become part of our society, learn the language! If the Union Jack offends you, or you don't like our Queen, then you should seriously consider a move to another part of the planet. We are happy with our culture and have no desire to change, and we really don't care how you did things where you came from. This is our country, our land, and our lifestyle.

'Our laws give every citizen the right to express their opinion, and we will allow you every opportunity to do so. But once you have finished complaining, whining, and griping about our flag, our government, or our way of life, I highly encourage you to take advantage of one other great British freedom, the right to leave. It is time for Great Britain to speak up. If you agree, pass this along. If you don't, delete it"...

All I can suggest is that you take the author's advice, whatever your opinion. As you can see, I've passed it along.

March 2006

ASK POLITELY NOW

Q: "WHAT DO WE WANT?"

A: "TO PULL OUT FROM THE EU!!!"

Q: "WHEN DO WE WANT IT?"

A: "NOW!!!"

Q: "AND WHAT DO WE SAY?"

A: "PLEASE"

Which is all very British. But as the EU's influence bites deeper, there will be real stirrings of fury. The 'regionalisation' of the Police and Fire Services (followed by the NHS) will throw fuel onto the fire, along with massive rises in Council Tax as County Councils are axed, along with counties themselves.

Devon, Cumbria, Norfolk etc, will remain as a polite fiction on a few signposts and guidebooks, but in reality they will be dead. In a few years time the Regional Assembly (agents of Brussels and the EU) will run the Regions and control the cash.

This is known as "The Westminster bypass" when everyone reading this will truly have become EU Citizens, with their own EU passport, biometric ID card, and EU national flag.

What a state to be in.

March 2006

SOIL DISASSOCIATION

When is organic not organic?

I'll tell you. When the European Union says so. A draft directive from Brussels has now recommended that GM contamination of organic food should be allowed up to a level of 1.9%. In other words the EU will allow contamination of your organic produce, rather than defending an industry that has doubled its sales in the last five years and will probably do much better in years to come.

Organic farming responds to the market, encouraging townies into the countryside to visit farm shops, to buy locally-produced food, and bringing money into the rural economy... It's also one of the few areas of farming that hardly benefits from the Common

Agricultural Policy, which currently costs every adult in Britain £250 a year in higher taxes and food prices, hitting the poorest hardest.

The Globalisation Institute - an independent think-tank – recently praised Prince Charles for his support of organic farming, saying that the CAP has been: "a disaster for the countryside and that taxation used to fund it is theft from the common people".... The Institute went on: "The Prince of Wales has given us a vision of a countryside concentrating not on high output but on high quality, high value produce".

One more interesting fact. ***The EU has now forced health food manufacturers to prove that their vitamins and minerals are safe.*** But with big-lobbying GM groups like Monsanto - an industry unable to find a market - they can peddle their snake poison **unless it is proven dangerous.** This is a terrible double standard, showing the moral bankruptcy of the EU.

For everyone who chooses to buy organic food it seems that the definition of what is organic no longer resides with the Soil Association nor with Westminster. The decision will now be made in Brussels, whether we like it or not.

This is what they mean by 'loss of sovereignty'.

March 2006

THE OFFSIDE RULE EXPLAINED

During the 1996 European Championships, the Daily Mirror's headline was: "Achtung! Surrender – For you Fritz ze European Championships are over", above a photo of footballers Gazza and Stuart Pearce in tin hats with "We will fight them on the flanks, fight them on the midfield" etc, though fortunately editor Piers Morgan stopped short of "We must fight them on the terraces". A Mirror reporter sneaked into the swimming pool of the German team's training ground and draped Mirror towels all over the poolside loungers. Morgan even planned to dive-bomb the German team's training ground with a Spitfire, dropping front pages of that day's edition.

Predictably the BBC howled with outrage, and the Sunday Times, Guardian and Spectator all followed up with articles of foaming condemnation against editor Mr Morgan. Bobby Charlton called him "thick".

On the other hand, the Germans reacted differently, sending Morgan a note: "Achtung! For you Britz ze world cup, ze Ashes und ze Empire alles Kaput!" while the German-British Consortium awarded him the booby prize for Least Constructive Contribution to Anglo-German relations of the Year" (one of his sub editors went to collect the prize, explaining that although he'd co-written the article he was "only obeying orders.")

In the meantime Morgan sent a Harrods food hamper around to Jurgen Klinsmann, the German captain, as a peace offering: the photo in the next day's Mirror was headlined "PEAS IN OUR TIME" because there were frozen peas in the hamper. As Morgan said in his superb book The Insider: "Why do the Germans all find it funny, but the British have all had a collective sense of humour failure? I'm baffled."

I can tell him. It's not the Germans who lack the sense of humour. It's us...The political class, at least, have lost it in a stew of sanctimonious political correctness. Imagine turning up at the BBC with the script of Fawlty Towers under your arm: "You'll like this. I'll do the silly walk"...

"Thank you, Mr Cleese. We'll be in touch".

March 2006

WHEN DANGER REARED ITS UGLY HEAD

There is something wrong with our Armed Forces. But please don't take it from me. Take it from Colonel Tim Collins, whose speech to his men on the eve of the invasion of Iraq inspired the world.

In an article in The Times (12/10/05) Col Collins said that British forces in Iraq and Afghanistan were being put at risk by a cohort of officers more interested in their careers than in fighting: "One particular little red, fat general has never been in a fight in a playground. He's a civilian soldier in the true sense of never letting anything happen... When we find ourselves in a shooting war, not only are these chaps at sea but they are frantic to survive. There's a conflict at the heart of the Army. It's almost a congenital condition."

Col Collins then discussed the ongoing creation of the European Army, which is already well underway. The proposed scrapping of the tried and tested regimental system would come with a blood price: "There's no reason why a European Army should do the extraordinary things that regiments do. That will be the cause of the first great defeat of the British Army. You will see guys running away. There's no reason to stay. There's no Black Watch or Royal Irish or whatever. It's just a European Army."

March 2006

NEVER FIT AN ALUMINIUM SUMP-GUARD BENEATH YOUR ENGINE, AND OTHER USEFUL TIPS FOR MOTORING IN THE DESERT

In February 2005...along with co-driver Ralph Gay, I drove an old banger in the Plymouth/Dakar Rally 3,000-miles down through Europe and across to Morocco, Western Sahara etc to The Gambia. For the record we had a great time, raised £1,000 for "Direct" the diabetes charity, and despite virtually trashing the car en-route still managed to sell it for £950 in the auction ring in Banjul (the cash went to local charities down there).

The reason I'm telling you this is partly to thank the MEP Graham Booth (UKIP) who privately helped sponsor us, and Bruce Robertson, boss of Trago, who also put in money. There were others and many thanks to you all.

Down in a place called Dakla we were parked outside the only 5-star hotel (we weren't residents, I hasten to add) when a lovely lady named "Fuzzy", from Helston in Cornwall, also on the Rally, approached the car, homing in on the TRAGO MILLS stickers emblazoned across bonnet, boot, and doors.

We got talking with Fuzzy and I mentioned that I wrote this column. Her reply was: "So *you're* David Challice. I think the Trago Column is *brilliant*."...

Just as I was puffing myself up like Mr Toad, she added: "Of course, I don't agree with you. I like being in Europe, but I love your stuff."

I think this is brilliant. An intelligent lady who is happy with the EU (though she wants to keep the pound and say "no" to the Constitution) but is happy reading a contrary view with an open mind without getting her undergarments in a twist. It's just a shame that the pro-EU lobby can't approach things in a similar way, without insults of xenophobia or of being a little Englander. One day maybe they'll learn.

April 2006

TELLING IT HOW IT IS

For an example of leadership with guts, try this one. On 8/2/06 in Canberra, Australia, Prime Minister John Howard told Muslims who want to live under Sharia law that Australia was not the place for them. Following a meeting with mainstream Muslims, the Government made it clear that Australia was a secular state and its laws were made by parliament.

Treasurer, Peter Costello, told national television: "If those are not your values, if you want a country which has Sharia law or a theocratic state, then Australia is not for you. I'd be saying to clerics who are teaching that there are two laws governing people in Australia, one the Australian law and another the Islamic law, that this is false."

Education Minister Brendon Nelson made it even clearer, telling local reporters: "Basically, people who don't want to be Australians, and they don't want to live by Australian values and understand them, well they can basically clear off."

Contrast this with the appeasement policy of American and European governments to the recent Islamic cartoons that appeared in a Danish newspaper, which themselves only appeared after an author writing a children's book could not find an illustrator brave enough to depict the Prophet. The murderous threats from some Muslims has proved how correct those fears were. Some of the cartoons were added later by Revolutionary Islamists.

The British, European and American governments should be listening to the messages coming from Australia. This is real, blunt, unequivocal leadership, sorely lacking in many capital cities at the moment, and we are the losers for that fact.

April 2006

DON'T USE IT AS A RULE

Those who love the metre and are itching to ditch the yard (calling it antiquated and unscientific) should bear something in mind. Metric was introduced 200 years ago by a bunch of revolutionary hotheads who became very handy with Madame la' Guillotine. At the time, prominent French scientists such as Pierre Laplace warned them that their metric system was defective, inadequate, and based on unsound principles; but rather like the EU today they were deaf to criticism.

Ancient units of measurement (the yard, pole, link, fathom, furlong, foot) are all related to the natural world by a compatible time-distance ratio. In other words they connect us with the physical earth that exists around us as we spin through space. For example, the Anglo Saxon rod (6.6ft or 79.2 inches) relates to a ten millionth part of half the earth's circumference and coincides with the 12-hour clock. And if you subtract the 360 degrees of the earth's circumference from the 43,560 sq ft of the acre you are left with 43,200, exactly the number of seconds in 12 hours.

Pre-revolutionary France had a perfectly good measuring system. Their own version of the fathom was the Toise de Perou standard, with 864 lines (lignes) in every six feet (pieds). They used 864 'lignes' because there are 86,400 seconds in a 24-hour time span. The Revolutionaries could have chosen a scientific approach by adopting Mouton's milliare (a nautical mile) and making the metre the equivalent of the Anglo Saxon rod (79.20 inches), which is a 1/10,000,000th part of the length of the equator, the distance the earth moves in exactly 12 hours.

Instead they invented a new metric measurement, which is an imposed man-made system, relating to nothing more than an arbitrary political decision taken at the time. Because metric did not relate distance to time, both Jefferson and Adams in the USA rejected it as unscientific and chose Imperial.

Even the defined measurement of the metre is itself inaccurate. The French came up with a value of 1/10,000,000th as a quarter of the earth's circumference, making the metre equal to 39.37 inches. But this was wrong, because they had measured the earth incorrectly. The true metre should measure 39.6 inches, meaning that the present metre is 0.23 inches short, equating to 2ft in every kilometre....

To sum up, British Governments have progressively surrendered our ancient system of measurements which have worked perfectly well for centuries and are still used by the world's No.1 superpower (the USA). At no time did anyone tell the British people of this, still less ask them. Anyone who objects is subject to refutation by denigration, branded a fool or crank, or hopelessly old fashioned, with a finger tapping the head, accompanied by cartoon 'cuckoo music'. As a result, we now have a metric system which relates to nothing in the world around us, apart from one calculation which turns out to be wrong.

Call me foolish, cranky or loony but this doesn't seem a terribly good deal.

April 2006

IT'S GREAT TO BE BACK ON TERRA COTTA

In a strange and uncanny sense, it is almost a privilege to be around whilst New Labour is in power, because never in our lifetime have we seen a more utterly useless shower at the helm (this even includes John Major's lot, which is saying something).

We have John Prescott, deputy prime minister, who calls himself middle class, but is only there to reassure the Unions and Labour's traditional working class vote. Even his own father said: "John will be working class 'till the day he dies": and listening to the interview one could almost hear him add affectionately: "the great Jessie."

Mr Prescott's latest gaffe has become a classic: "If you set up a school and it becomes a good school the great danger is that everyone wants to go there."

But he's not alone. The Citizenship Minister, Tony Mc Nulty, was asked on BBC2's Newsnight about the estimated 300,000 immigrants who have recently flooded into Britain from the new EU countries in eastern Europe. His department had originally predicted 13,000 or so. Mr McNulty's priceless contribution was: "We can't plan for the future". In true New Labour-land style, he was presumably planning for the past.

Shuffling up next for the gaffe-stakes was ill-suited Home Secretary, Charles Clarke, on Radio 4's Today programme in February. He had already proposed that prison inmates sign a contract promising to behave themselves. In return the Government would find them accommodation when they were released.

The Today programme interviewed an ex-con who ridiculed the idea, saying that no prisoner she had ever met would trust the Government's word. Mr Clarke's timeless response was: "Well, you don't expect me to take the word of a convicted criminal." In which case, why ask convicted criminals to sign the contracts in the first place?

April 2006

COME IN NUMBER 6, YOUR TIME IS UP

There was a TV show in the 1960s called The Prisoner, starring Patrick McGoohan. At the time it was a bit of a flop, though as word spread it eventually became a cult hit around the world. The hero, No 6, was a disgruntled spy who slammed down his resignation on the boss's desk and soon found himself waking up at "The Village", a place where individualism is banned. Hence the famous line: "I am not a number; I am a free man!" which was greeted by derisory laughter from whoever happened to be No2 that week.

At the time The Prisoner was too wacky for the mainstream, but now it seems horribly accurate. If you think I'm over-exaggerating (and you were thinking that, weren't you?) then get hold of one of the episodes and judge for yourself. It is oddly spooky and

I can easily imagine the EU (or even New Labour) dreaming up a similar establishment within a few years time.

John Prescott, or even Patricia Hewitt (bless her) would make great No2's. The dialogue is already written for them. For example, take this line from the script: "Questions are a burden for others. Answers are a prison to oneself," though Mr Prescott would probably muddle his lines.

From the government that banned smoking in pubs and working men's clubs - without a mandate - and an EU that loses a referendum on the Constitution and then goes ahead and brings it in by the back door, anything – virtually anything - is possible.

May 2006

A BUCKET OF WINDFALLS

I'm not sure what to write about this week. Not the EU again, and certainly not Cameron or his double Blair. It all gets a bit tedious at times. Collective nouns, perhaps? There must be some mileage in "a Parliament of Owls" or " Building of Rooks" or "Murder of Crows". But no, that's not really going to get us very far.

How about recent howlers of English usage? "He lead me up the garden path", or "I expect everyone to tow the Party line", or "He poured over his book". But nope, that's pretty awful too. Perhaps I'm losing the touch. (Just between the two of us, I can't wait to see where this is going).

Maybe things will get moving if we try something different. What have we got in the clippings box? Ah, here's one. An article in the Australian Times revealing that 150,000 middle-class Aussies in 2006, fed up with long hours, urban stress, crime and traffic jams, have now fled to the Outback in pursuit of the rural dream. One city broker gave up his £60,000 job and bought a ranch down an eight-mile track. "We love it", said his wife. "We miss things like restaurants, and we've been known to go on a 90-mile round trip for a Thai takeaway. But we're so much more laid back. We love listening to the radio and hearing about the traffic congestion in Sydney."

The 'gentle irony' here is that many newcomers are also bringing their urban values with them. One academic, from the centre of social research at Woomera University, said: "People complain about the smells from farms and the noise of tractors driving at night. Chooks (chickens) going off every morning at 5am can be a bit confronting."

There, I knew we'd probably arrive somewhere interesting if I only kept going. I just hope you think it was worth the journey.

May 2006

A LITTLE BROTHER FOR GALILEO

The only thing George Orwell got wrong was the date...You might be interested to know that the EU is pressing ahead with a space satellite system called "Global Monitoring for Environment and Security" or GMES, which should be up and running by 2010.

Brussels has already acknowledged that GMES will play a key role in the "implementation, review and monitoring of EU policies" ... Partly this is to watch for fraud from farmers or fishermen, but also to "provide authorities with necessary elements for a European Security and Defence Policy."

The USA is suspicious of Brussels' existing 30-satellite Galileo system because the Chinese have already been invited to become a major investor. In 2005 the USA stated that if they become seriously concerned at the military and security threat posed by Chinese involvement, then they will shoot down European satellites. So much for the EU securing peace in Europe.

Gregor Kreuzhuber, the commission's spokesman for industry policy, recently described GMES as: "a little brother for Galileo, a sort of satellite system where you can better monitor what is happening on our planet".

Among other plans for GMES is the introduction of a pan-European road-charging system, with a spy in every car. We will be paying for the privilege of keeping the EU informed of our whereabouts.

If you're happy about this then by all means carry on and vote for the Lib-Lab-Con at the next general election, whistle as you head along the primrose pathway. But ask yourself just one question: if Her Majesty's Official Opposition is meant to be a watchdog over our freedoms, why are they fast asleep with their chops in the food bowl? Why the silence, Mr Cameron?

May 2006

WASN'T YOUR'S A SCOTTISH CONSTITUENCY?

Last year Gordon Brown said we should all be waving the Union flag and celebrating our Britishness. There's only one problem. Britain has now been chopped up like the Balkans (thanks to New Labour and its EU regionalisation plan).

We have the Scottish Parliament, the Welsh Assembly, and (if the IRA can stop murdering people for long enough) a Northern Ireland Assembly. There will never be an English Parliament (nor a Cornish one, for those of you west of the Tamar) because it doesn't square with the big coloured map on the wall in Brussels.

The result of this regionalisation is that Britishness barely exists, in the sense of a general binding force holding us all together. Even our passport identifies us as EU citizens.

This leaves ethnic minorities in a quandary. They identify themselves as British Asians or British Moslems just when everybody else is dropping the idea of Britishness. And coming from a totally alien background and culture, it must be utterly bewildering for them... rather like arriving late at a party only to find that everyone has dispersed to the kitchen, sitting room and garden, and are now barely talking to one-another.

The Tories must share the blame for weakening the Union. In 1955 they took seats all over Scotland, with more than 50% of the vote. These days the expression 'Scottish Tory' is an oxymoron... the direct result of a naïve European dream that is rapidly becoming a nightmare.

June 2006

WELL-DRIVEN? CALL 999

On 31st March, David Cameron said... this: "At the heart of Labour's project for reform of local government is one word: Regionalism. Where this obsession with dividing England into large, remote regional blocs comes from is a matter for speculation. I'm not sure what the reason is."

I think I can help Mr Cameron with his problem, but I suspect he'll be clapping his hands over his ears and singing loudly to drown out the truth. The answer to his question is that 'Regionalism' comes from Brussels (full title The European Union of the Cities and Regions) and the Tories signed up to it in 1992 with the Maastricht Treaty. If a possible future prime minister can be so ignorant of the facts, then we're in bad trouble.

Just for the record, EU Regionalisation Policy means that all our County-based Police forces, ambulance services, fire brigades, and Crown and County Courts are to be regionalised. Even as I write this, the Chief Constable of Devon & Cornwall Police is fighting a brave but doomed rearguard action to save her force from being swallowed by a South West Regional Police Force.

May I end with a quote from the EU Commission in 1969 (and let's hope that David Cameron is reading this, and not off hugging icebergs somewhere)

"The EEC or the regions is to determine all economic and social policy and not the nation states...If member states remained responsible for regional policy then the development of the EEC would be jeopardised – harmonious economic development could not be left to the member states".

June 2006

NEWS FROM OUR MAN UNDER THE DUVET

You might be interested in Matthew Elliot's "The Bumper Book of Government Waste". Or perhaps you won't. It's a bit too depressing. Mr Elliot heads the Tax-payers' Alliance, which monitors Gordon Brown's spending, and he has unearthed some real gems. So bear these in mind when paying your Council Tax...

The new NHS computer system had an original budget of £6.3-billion, but will probably end up costing £50-billion (or five-thousand million pounds, the same amount of money the West wrote off African debt at last year's Live8 concert), whilst the £450-million IT system for the Child Support Agency went £50-million over budget and will continue to be an utter nightmare for anyone dealing with it.

Government departments also did their bit. The Dept. for Constitutional Affairs spends £9 million a year on outside consultants compared to £700,000 in 1997. One consultant is paid £2,100 a day.

Mere chickenfeed is the £2,500 granted to an RAF Aircraftwoman to re-train as a lap-dancer and stripper, or the £874,387 paid by the Metropolitan Police to patrol Abu Hamza's street meetings.

If you think this is bad (and it is) then the chapter on the EU will send you back under the duvet. For example, £1,900-million of Britain's annual contribution went to subsidise Continental European tobacco farmers "whose crop is so foul that Europeans refuse to smoke it." The EU also costs us £39-million every single day of the year.

The British Monarchy is the one positive note in all this: the net gain of our having a Royal Family is a contribution of £127-million to the national exchequer, by the Government's own figures. As Mr Elliot puts it: "Not only does it pay for itself, it buys everyone in the country a drink as well".

I don't know about you, but I certainly raise my glass to that.

June 2006

THINK AHEA

On the 7th of May 1915 a single German torpedo slammed into the British liner Lusitania and sent her to the bottom of the Atlantic. One of the passengers wrote a message and stuffed it into a bottle as the vessel was going down. The message finished: "THE END IS NEAR. MAYBE THIS NOTE WILL ..." which suggests that things had got a bit hectic.

If UKIP fails to pull Britain out of the EU (and we cannot do it without your help) then our eventual abandonment of the doomed European Project will be even more chaotic and dangerous than the escape of that un-named passenger from the sinking Lusitania.

On the subject of messages in bottles, Captain Harvey Bennet (a US coastguard from Long Island, New York) wrote his name and address in a plastic bottle and tossed it into the sea. A few months later the bottle was delivered back to him in the regular mail. Captain Bennet was delighted, until he read the note: "I found your bottle while taking a scenic walk by Poole Harbour. While you may consider this some profound experiment on the path and speed of oceanic currents, I have another name for it – litter. You Americans don't seem to be happy unless you are mucking up somewhere. If you wish to foul your own nest, all well and good. But please refrain from fouling mine!" The letter was signed by Henry Biggelsworth of Bournemouth.

Although I condemn littering, this seems rather churlish and miserable. Should I ever find myself aboard an ocean liner with Mr "B" when a U-boat sinks it, I must advise him not to climb onto my life-raft. I will be sorely tempted to heave him over the side and – like that plastic bottle – see how long it takes him to reach Poole Harbour. You may judge this a little severe, but I don't believe I'm being too hard on him.

June 2006

INFORM, EDUCATE, ENTERTAIN

I happen to like the BBC, and don't mind paying a licence fee (if you've ever watched American TV which can be defined as a series of adverts interrupted by the occasional programme, you'll know what I mean) but there is a huge problem with the culture at the heart of the Corporation.

It is no accident that BBC vacancies are advertised in the Guardian newspaper, because their editorial lines are virtually identical, a progressive-left slant that has skewed the Corporation and alienated the silent majority who pay the licence fee. Remember that this is a public service broadcaster with a legally binding charter, one which it frequently breaches.

Rik Mayall (star of the Young Ones, the Comic Strip, Bottom, and the New Statesman) is in no doubt. "To work at the BBC you have to be gay, black or a woman. British TV used to be the finest in the world. Now it's totally imploded" (The Sun 3/10/05).

It's not only Light Entertainment. The department of News and Current Affairs is even worse. When Radio 4's Today programme ran a listeners poll to decide who really runs Britain, the winner was EU President Barroso (three times the number who voted for Blair) leaving red faces in the editorial office. The same happened when Today ran a poll for a "Listener's Law". To their politically correct horror, a vast majority of listeners voted for householders to defend their property by force, the so-called "Tony Martin law". The Today programme had originally offered to help the winning selection on its way through Parliament, but quietly dropped its support when the result was announced.

As Godfrey Bloom MEP (UKIP) said: "A little less pathetic appeal to 'yoof' and more to middle-England who pick up the tab might enhance their prestige... After the Iraq war, of course, New Labour and the BBC have fallen out, as thieves will, but I suspect the ultra-left PC Lib-Dems have already filled the vacancies".

Though be warned: if you ring up the BBC's complaint line, they will pass you onto an 0870 number, charging 8p a minute. Which pretty much says it all really.

July 2006

PLEASE SIR

This one's about the British Constitution....

Yes, I know, but you'll just have to wake up and pay attention. It's like Shakespeare at school. Or maths. When it's over, you'll be glad you stuck with it. We'll go for a drink afterwards.

Right then. The Constitution. First, if a country doesn't have one, it ends up with a civil war or revolution because constitutions place a legal duty upon those who govern. That's why the barons forced King John to sign the Magna Charta in 1215. As the years passed others came along (Petition of Rights 1628, the Bill of Rights and the Coronation Oath, both 1689, and others like the Acts of Union 1707, that we needn't worry about here)... The point is that Britain does have a written Constitution, despite many claims that it does not. It's just that the Constitution is written in, basically, six documents.

Wake up at the back, please. Open a window if you must. If you think this is boring then just remember that the Bill of Rights forbids "Judicial Torture" or "Taxation Without Representation". What lies at the heart of the British Constitution is the Rule of Law, and everybody is subject to it. You, me, the Monarch, Parliament, the Prime Minister.

The idea that Parliament enjoys unfettered power - that the divine right of kings somehow morphed into a divine right of parliament - is simply wrong. The whole purpose of the Constitution is to ensure that people are never again to be repressed. The phrase "An Englishman is born a free man save under the due restraint of the necessary law" resonates the world over, and...Oh, and there's the bell.

Those joining me for post-lesson ale, we meet in the bar in five minutes. The rest of you, homework is to contact John Bingley, at Chapel Cottage, Hoe Lane, Flansham, Sussex, PO22 8NT for in-depth details of the written British Constitution.

And please remember that this is **part of the syllabus and you will *certainly be tested on this next summer***.

July 2006

"I AM HAPPY"

It's very important to be happy...not irritatingly up-
beat, or grinning like an imbecile overdue for
professional care. Just pretty contented with life and
with ones own position in it. Ask David Cameron. He
thinks we should all concentrate on health not wealth,
and in fairness he's probably right.

The problem with being born rich, is that nothing is
ever a treat. What do you give a man who has always
had everything? Penicillin, I suppose.

A poll in the 1950s showed that 52% of Britons said
they were "Very Happy". The figure has now dropped
to 32%, despite the fact that we're three times richer.
A bigger house or car doesn't seem to be the answer.
Or if it is, perhaps we're asking the wrong question.

It's rather like the anti-EU stance. Questioning the EU
once implied that you were - to quote Tony Blair - "a
swivel-eyed extremist". Things have changed, as they
always do. Many professional academics are now
joining the "anti" camp, recognising that it's worth
sacrificing their chances of becoming a fellow of the
British Academy, a vice-chancellor, or an emeritus
professor; all for the pure joy, the sheer unalloyed
relief, the simple happiness in fact, of uttering the
truth.

Now that's something to smile about.

July 2006

AND STILL SMILING

Last week I did a piece on HAPPINESS, but it's a big subject. Although I'm no Buddhist, I thought you might be interested in the Dalai Lama's view of our Western happiness (or lack of it), this from an interview he gave to journalist Alice Thomson in April 2006...

"It is fascinating", he reflected in his slightly stilted English. "In the West you have bigger homes, yet smaller families. You have endless conveniences – yet you never seem to have any time. You can travel anywhere in the world, yet you don't bother to cross the road to meet your neighbours.... I don't think people have become more selfish, but their lives have become easier and that has spoilt them. They expect more, they constantly compare themselves to others and they have too much choice – which brings no real freedom... The West is now quite weak – it can't cope with adversity and has little compassion for others. People are like plants: they can develop ways of countering negative forces. If people took more responsibility for their own problems they would become more self-confident".

You may disagree, but I think he's got a point.

On a more international note, the Dalai Lama recently met George Bush at the White House and was very impressed by the President's straightforwardness and grasp of Buddhism. "Bush offered me his favourite biscuit and after that we got on fine." But when asked about Tony Blair, he restricted himself to the words: "He smiles a lot."

I think he's got a point there, too.

July 2006

STRANGERS INTO CITIZENS

Back in the Fourth Century AD hundreds of thousands of Goth refugees were driven westwards by the Huns. The Roman Empire, aghast at this tidal wave of humanity, granted them asylum in Turkey. But this was a mistake, because in AD376 those same Goths then poured across the Danube in rafts, boats, and hollowed-out tree trunks. Awaiting them on the riverbank were corrupt Roman officials, who let them pass through to the Empire in return for payment in gold.

The historian Ammianus Marcellinus - serving as a frontier soldier at the time - wrote about the event years later: "Diligent care was taken that no future destroyer of the Roman State should be left behind, even if he were smitten with a fatal disease. With such stormy eagerness on the part of insistent men was the ruin of the Roman world brought in."

Our present asylum and immigration system (dominated by EU law and the Human Rights Act signed by Tony Blair in 1997) has uncanny echoes of that long-gone Roman world, especially the sense of disbelief among the populace at what is happening. Today we are unable to deport Afghan terrorist hi-jackers who have had their asylum appeals denied (and remember that Afghanistan is now a democracy).

Furthermore, convicted EU citizens cannot be deported from Britain at the end of their sentence because that contravenes their free movement throughout the Union. There are currently 12 million more National Insurance numbers in the UK system than there are people. One unsubstantiated source (claiming to be from within the Dept of Work & Pensions itself) informs me that in fact there is a total of 120-million NI numbers in existence. Given that in our population of 70-million, perhaps 50-million are likely to have a number, the figure of 120-million seems incredible......... and therefore is very possibly true.

Since 2003 untold thousands of illegal immigrants were granted tax credits by the Inland Revenue when their asylum application had been rejected, all because we need low-paid street-sweepers. Call me pernickety but this is not an immigration policy. It's a dog's breakfast.

When the Government (or even a Tory government) blathers away about crime, immigration, or terrorism, remember that they have already surrendered control to Brussels, which now makes 80% of our laws. They have cornered the market in hot air and incompetence.

Ammianus Marcellinus must be looking down, shaking his head, and smiling wearily.

August 2006

LICKING YOUR OWN ELBOW

As a change from targeting the EU, let's do something different. In Ancient Babylon it was an established tradition that for one lunar month after a wedding the bride's father would supply his new son-in-law with all the mead he could drink. Mead comes from honey, hence "honeymoon"...Interesting? Don't worry; there's more.

Ale in English taverns was served in pints and quarts. When things got rowdy the landlord would shout:

"Mind your P's and Q's and settle down, gentlemen, please!"...And some ceramic beer-jugs had a whistle baked into the handle, which was used to attract the barman's attention. In other words, to "wet your whistle".

It is impossible to lick your elbow (but apparently 75% of you will now try).

Women can hear better than men, but men can read smaller print (which might explain why women can't read maps). Ahem. Moving swiftly on.

In Medieval English houses (often little more than thatched huts) most floors were made of compacted earth, hence "dirt poor". The wealthy had stone floors that became slippery when wet, so they laid down straw (or 'thresh') underfoot. To prevent passing feet taking it back outside they laid a strip of wood across the doorway - the "threshold".

Still in the medieval kitchen, it was a sign of the family's wealth if they could obtain pork, so they hung up a side of bacon to impress visitors, proving that the man of the house could "bring home the bacon". Then they would cut off a strip and sit around with their guests "chewing the fat". As for bread, it was apparently divided according to status. The burnt bottom part was given to the workers of the house. High status visitors got "the upper crust".

Finally, you might be interested in hearing about the job of the man who had to sit outside the churchyard the night after a funeral lest an apparent corpse awoke in the coffin. This rang a bell above the grave during the "graveyard shift", and with a bit of luck led to a "dead ringer" being "saved by the bell".

(If there's anybody out there still reading this), that's enough interesting facts for now. Next week, back to Brussels.

August 2006

HOPELESSLY PROGRESSIVE

"Progress" has been described as a small child clutching the reins of a runaway carriage as it hurtles downhill with no brakes. A quick look at history proves that theory.

Take Easter Island in the Pacific Ocean. The inhabitants became caught up in a bizarre God-cult rivalry, felling all the forests to erect their vast statues. In his book 'A Short History of Progress', Ronald Wright describes the end: "The people who felled that last tree could see it was the last, could know with complete certainty that there would never be another. And they felled it anyway" The moral of the story is that you can never make things idiot-proof because the idiots are always one step ahead. ***But at least you can try.***

A good example is our fishing industry, currently being crucified by the EU. If we were running it we might just have a chance of success. During the Second World War our fish were pretty much left alone, thanks to Hitler's U-boats. Incredibly, by 1945, stocks were six-times higher than in 1940. But within three years they had plunged back to pre-war levels through over-fishing. So, firm Government control is vital, even if some fishermen don't like it (But most of them are French or Spanish and do not count).

There is a lesson here. New Zealand recently

announced 'fallow areas' in her territorial waters, with great success. And we could do the same. But not from within the EU and its Common Fisheries Policy where perfectly good fish are thrown overboard because it's a Thursday and the skipper has already caught his quota of half-a-dozen plaice.

The only way to save our fisheries and preserve stocks is for us to leave the EU and run the industry properly. Please do not expect the Tories to do this, despite their honeyed words. David Cameron has recently dropped his Party's commitment to "repatriating" our fishing grounds. This is the equivalent of that small child throwing away the reins, cupping his chin in one hand, and watching the ensuing smash with detached interest.

August 2006

A EURO-VISION

I have a confession to make: *I watch the Eurovision Song Contest.*

Some things have changed over the years. The bizarre quirkiness, the sequins, flared-trousers and tragic hairstyles have all pretty much gone; though viewers from the Crab Nebula probably feel that Europe is still too wacky for a holiday destination just yet. But in fact, they would be wrong. 'Eurovision', sadly, has become almost professional, and I speak as one who knows.

Some things, thankfully, haven't changed at all. The French sing an identical song every year (in French) and do not win; the Viking-States all vote for each other; the British entry limps in at fifteenth, and yet again we are all too polite to ask how **Israel**, that well known European country, ever came to be invited.

Most interestingly, the voting now overtly involves politics and diplomacy. Montenegro won't vote for Serbia; Serbia won't vote for Croatia; therefore Montenegro votes for Croatia, to show solidarity. Or as journalist Ed West once said: "The Cypriot entry could simply walk on stage and belch, and still be sure of twelve points from the Greeks".

This also explains why France, Germany and Britain will probably never win again. Small states vote to show support for their neighbours. Large, important states, being strong, do not need to make gestures, and are unlikely to take offence and invade, say, Latvia, for not voting for 'Chirpy-Booma-Bang'. The British, at least, treat Eurovision as a huge joke.

The sobering question is that if the Eurovision Song Contest is so blatantly up the junction what in the name of blue blazes are we doing in its big brother, the European Union?

September 2006

YOU READ IT HERE FIRST

If you're one of those who think that Gordon Brown would make a great Prime Minister then we're about to part company. Mr Brown is certainly a clever man, and very lucky, but he has single-handedly destroyed Britain's pensions industry, and for that he can never be forgiven.

In 1997 he was warned that taxing private pensions would rob funds of £12-billion. Following a Freedom of Information request by the Daily Mail newspaper,

Treasury archive documents clearly show that Mr Brown realised that he could increase his coffers by £11.6-billion in the first two years, all at the expense of pensions savers. The Treasury pinned their hopes on a rise in the stock market to plug the gap. Instead share prices plummeted in 2001/2002, and the proverbial hit the revolving air-agitator.

We now have a crisis leaving huge shortfalls in pensions, forcing hundreds of firms to wind up their final salary schemes, all caused by this apparently prudent Chancellor. In December 2005 the Pensions Commission (headed by Lord Turner) warned: "Voluntary private pension provision is not growing; rather it is in serious and irreversible decline".

If an orderly transition of power in New Labour results in this man ever becoming Prime Minister (something that remains in doubt) then leave the door unlocked when you leave. It saves the squatters damaging the mechanism when they arrive.

September 2006

In summer 2007 it became front-page news that Brown had been warned that his actions would cripple the UK pensions industry. Very odd. Had they subscribed to the Trago Column, they would have known months earlier.

OUTSIDE FOR A BREATH OF FRESH AIR

Every now and again I realise that God has a great sense of humour and is looking down on this world, studying the race He created, and chuckling to Himself at the absurdities of which we are capable. I don't mean the big things; the wars, the famines, etc. I mean the small things, the petty things.

Take Adam Pressman, a menswear manager in Exeter. He was having a drink in a city wine bar when he went outside for a hand-rolled cigarette. He finished the cigarette, dropped it, put it out with his foot. He was immediately fined £75 by a waiting Litter Enforcement Officer who had been watching him.

I don't condone littering, but even a speeding ticket is only £60, and the hate-war that is being waged against otherwise law-abiding smokers is actually driving people out into the street where ashtrays are not plentiful. And you can bet your last euro that the City Councils won't put the same effort into tackling the burger/fried chicken-and-vomit wrappers littering the city streets on a Friday and Saturday night; too much of a possibility that some drunken yob will lay one on the Litter Enforcement staff, so the authorities will concentrate on the easy targets, those who drop a bio-degradable cigarette butt in their lunch hour.

In 2004 these anti-smoking measures were being pushed through the EU Parliament (That's right, it's Brussels again. Couldn't you guess?). Three of UKIP's MEPs attended a lunch there. At the end of the meal those on the top table sat back, pushed away their pudding plate and lit up cigarettes. Graham Booth MEP interrupted them: "Excuse me, Gentlemen. Haven't you seen the notice?" He indicated the NO SMOKING sign literally above their heads... Their response was: "Oh, get a life!"

And this from a bunch of politicians in Brussels who had just voted on legislation affecting British smokers. This hypocrisy is like rotten mackerel by moonlight; it shines and stinks. Sorry, but it's time we governed ourselves.

October 2006

GETTING RIGHT UP DAVID MILIBAND

I always enjoy absurdities. Here's one now, a letter to the newspapers from Graham Watson, Lib Dem MEP: ***"The best way to protect British jobs is to get Britain into the Euro – fast!"*** This classic is now framed on my office wall.

There are others. Take Tom Williams from SPLASH clothing, who was given an £80 fixed penalty ticket for selling T-shirts bearing the slogan "Bollocks to Blair". This was at the Royal Show, Stoneleigh, Warwickshire; and the policemen involved demanded to know his eye colour, shoe-size, and National Insurance number, in case he did it again. The shirts had offended David Miliband, Environment Secretary, who was also at the show.

As Mr Williams said: "I personally find it offensive for young girls to go round in T-shirts with FCUK written on them. Perhaps we should spell it 'Bollokes to Blair'?"

Or try this one. Tory Shadow Transport spokesman, Chris Grayling, admitting that they'd messed up Rail Privatisation: "We think with hindsight that the complete separation of track and train into separate businesses at the time of privatisation was not right for our railways."

The problem is that the separation of track and train came from Brussels and is contained in Council Directive 91/440/EEC of 29th July 1991 on the Development of the Community's Railways.

One final absurdity. In February 2006 UKIP forced a vote in the EU Parliament on retaining the pint and other imperial measures. We won by 448 to 89. Without us pushing for it, Britain would have lost the pint of beer. But **Conservative MEP Giles Chichester voted against us and against keeping the British pint.** Now why would he do that?

The Tories. Safe on Europe? Do me a favour.

October 2006

NOT IN MY NAME

I had a good belly laugh in June, courtesy of an article in The Western Morning News. The item highlighted a Mr Hawkins who had publicly dropped to his knees, chains on his wrists, wearing the T-shirt "SO SORRY", begging forgiveness from The Gambia for the sins of his slave-trading ancestor, Sir John Hawkins.

Where does all this stop? Should Bristol pay an annual 'slavery levy' because the city grew fat on the slave trade? Or do we demand grovelling apologies from Paris because the Normans won in 1066 and grabbed all the best castles, giving us the British Class System as an added bonus? Or perhaps we should go back a couple of millennia and demand damages from Rome because Julius Caesar came, saw, and did a little shopping? (or vini, vide, visa).

Denmark and Norway must also pay up. The Danes and Vikings ran wild in the Dark Ages, treating the principles of sexual and cultural equality with disdain. The Guardian newspaper would have carried some very stiff editorials on the subject.

Madrid must also dig deep into her purse, for all the mental turmoil caused by the Spanish Armada. Speaking personally, the game of bowls has never really felt the same since my old history lessons. A sense of brooding unease lurks over the game.

And in the case of Sir John Hawkins, please bear in mind that African tribes preyed on their own neighbours, bringing them as captive slaves to the coast, where the waiting White men paid in hard goods for them. It takes two to tango, and slavery was a business transaction, involving Europeans and Africans. Therefore compensation will also be sought from modern African nations for all those Christian missionaries who went into the cooking pot.

Slavery is horrible. But how curiously politically-correct it is, judging a historical figure like Sir John Hawkins by the standards of today. It is a better use of our time and money to fight the modern version (sex trade and people trafficking) rather than navel-gazing about events that happened centuries ago, all totally beyond the control of anyone alive on the planet today.

If you persist in making a slavery-apology, you won't be doing it in my name.

November 2006

THE POST DEMOCRATIC PHASE

I'll try to keep this one short, but it's a huge subject, and quite detailed. The EU is not simply a political project to be run by a sort of Platonic council of wise men in Brussels (the Commission). The EU thinks of itself like that, of course. Peter Mandelson told us so himself: "Europe is now entering the post-Democratic phase". But there is another angle, and you might be interested in it.

As with all big schemes, people soon disagree and form into factions and start plotting away, undermining and stabbing each other in the back.

The EU is no different. One faction has a vision of the Commission running the show, with the member states meekly taking orders. But other groups reject this. They see the Commission as merely the Civil Service, with the real power held by the European Council (to which every member state sends a representative).

What is happening right now is a secret power struggle at the heart of the EU with these two factions vying for control of the wheel. They both want a United States of Europe; they both reject the Nation State, and they both hate political parties such as UKIP because it has the absolute luxury of telling you the truth about what is really going on in Brussels.

It strikes me that it doesn't matter who gets control of the wheel, because the road leads straight off a cliff and the brightest action is to bale out now. Right now. And the more one learns about this, the harder it is to disagree.

November 2006

ROBIN PAGE'S LEATHER JACKET

Bill Oddie (on last year's BBC Naturewatch) mentioned that jackdaws are now becoming scarce in the countryside. Jackdaws eat leatherjackets (or Daddy-Longlegs) that in turn live in cowpats. But a quick spin through the countryside in your car should explain the scarcity of leatherjackets. A field of cows is now worth a letter to the Times. No cows means no cowpats, and no pats means no leatherjackets.

May I quickly tell you about one of Robin Page's cows? Robin is a countryman, writes for The Daily

Telegraph, and presented One Man And His Dog, before the BBC became totally PC, and axed him.

Robin's cow was called Cherie (named after you know who) and had calved during the night, chasing Robin out of the field in the darkness.

In the morning he heard bellowing in the field and ran down to see what had happened. The calf was lying dead and Cherie had had a serious prolapse of the uterus. The vet came and shot her. As Robin said: "She may have been a protective fierce cow, but she was also in beautiful condition and watching animals die that have been with you for years is hard."

He could not give the beast to the local Cambridgeshire Hunt because she was over 24 months old (a BSE risk!). And because of absurd EU rules he couldn't bury her on his own land. So after endless useless phone calls to Defra, he himself eventually found a carrier to take the dead animal for incineration.

Robin takes up the story: *"I suppose you're taking her down the road?"*

"Oh no, they haven't got the contract" replied the driver, *"their concrete is cracked. I'm taking it to Somerset".*

So an old cow dies in Cambridgeshire and under waste regulations she has to be carted all the way to Somerset to be burnt? Global warming? Road congestion? Red tape? There is far more than concrete that is cracked. The world has gone mad."

Robin, I couldn't agree more.

December 2006

GOING TO MAURITIUS

The other day I asked: "Am I not master in my own house?" and the family – including cats – looked at me in amused silence. This proved something, to me at least. Trying to control your own affairs is like trying to drink from a water cannon, rather like the things happening in Britain today that are driving our own people abroad.

I'd like to quote from a letter I received in August, from a resigning UKIP member:

"I have sold my former house, the proceeds to be used as my pension fund in Mauritius, where I shall be taking early retirement... Actually I am very happy to be leaving this country, though I plan to return every two years to visit family and friends. I know of at least three families who have emigrated because they felt that this country was no longer a fit place to raise children, what with the "anything goes" policies now in place, which have seen the destruction of so much of what used to be our social fabric and public morals."

The writer went on: "In Mauritius the schoolchildren can be seen walking hand in hand, laughing and chatting happily as they walk to school, without their parents worrying that some maniac will molest or murder them.... Basically I wish UKIP every success, but the tide of licence and political correctness, I fear, is probably here for good. Time to jump ship!"

I would never criticise the writer for his personal decision. It's up to him. As for me, I'm here for the duration. I like the wind and the rain and the mud of England on my boots. The only reason I'm in UKIP is because it's the only chance we have left. For the sake of our country, I ask you to remember that at every single election.

December 2006

THE FENN STREET GANG

There are basically two ways to speak and write in Britain.

Latinate and Germanic. "Fancy talk" or "Anglo Saxon", and it goes back to 1066 when the Normans came over and grabbed all the top jobs and best castles. (The Working Class are pretty much Anglo Saxon... If you doubt this, try cutting up an HGV at the next roundabout, and you'll understand).

Both forms have enriched our language, but the Latinate has triumphed in Education and Government bureaucracy. And now we're all pulling out our hair.

Try this one for size: "In the articulatory transmission of information in an education situation the function of an effective teacher-communication which aims for broad culture-value similarity, and not exclusivity and multiformity, may be impeded by out-dated elitist conceptions."

It sounds like a Monty Python sketch, but comes from a 1999 Dept of Education document, and the twit who wrote it should never be allowed within 500-yards of any school, college, or university, let alone be employed at the tax-payer's expense.

I cannot speak for UKIP on matters of Education, but I will promise you this: We will "dustbin" this sort of crass, illiterate, insulting trash, and tell you how it is. You deserve more than you're getting.

December 2006

SPEAKING WORDS OF WISDOM

This is a shortened version of a lecture given in Washington DC in November 2006, by Dick Lamm, former governor of Colorado. Even if you disagree you might be interested in reading an opposing viewpoint (unless, of course, you have entirely succumbed to political correctness).

Lamm said: "If you believe that America is too smug, too self-satisfied, too rich; then let's destroy America. It's not that hard. Arnold Toynbee observed that 'an autopsy of history would show that all great nations commit suicide'. Here is how to do it...

'First, turn America into a multilingual and bicultural country. No nation can survive the tension and conflict of two competing languages or cultures. It is a blessing for an individual to be bilingual; however it is a curse for a society to be bilingual.

'Second, invent 'multiculturalism' and encourage immigrants to maintain their culture. Celebrate diversity, rather than emphasising our similarities. Make it an article of belief that all cultures are equal and that black and Hispanic dropout rates are due solely to prejudice and discrimination by the majority. Every other explanation is out of bounds.

'My next point for destroying America would be to get big foundations and businesses to give these efforts a lot of money. I would invest in 'victimology' and start a grievance industry blaming all minority failure on the majority population. And I would place all subjects off limits; make it taboo to talk against the cult of 'diversity'. I would find a word similar to 'heretic' in the 16th Century – that stopped discussion and paralysed thinking. Words like 'racist' or 'xenophobe' halt discussion and debate. And I would enforce a mantra: that because immigration has been good for America, it must always be good.'

Governor Lamm resumed his seat in silence. Every American in that room knew that everything he had said was proceeding methodically, quietly, darkly, yet pervasively.

It all sounds horribly familiar to what has happened here at home.

December 2006

2007

STIRRINGS FROM NORTH DEVON

Last autumn the Press Officer for Bideford Labour Party...yes, I thought that too. I hadn't realised it was so big... wrote to the newspapers complaining about UKIP.

She accused us of nostalgia for a British Empire when we "outsailed, outgunned, and outran our neighbours", and my response to that is "Yup, dead right". Outgunning the enemy is useful when fighting wars in Afghanistan or Iraq. Ask the troops. Or ask Tony Blair. And isn't the whole idea of the Olympic Games that we "outrun" our neighbours? Gold medals?

As for Empires, they rise and fall like the tide, and ours has now evolved into The Commonwealth. UKIP believes that we shouldn't hitch ourselves to the EU, this newest wannabee Empire, whose Parliament building in Strasburg is a deliberate (and publicly admitted) copy of the Tower of Babel. Even the architect-designed 'scaffolding' around the building is meant to signify "unfinished work".

Back to the Press Officer from Bideford's Labour Party machine. Taking time out from her hectic schedule, she blazed on: "It seems ironic that UKIP sends MEPs to Brussels when it is trying to destroy that institution. Perhaps it's something to do with the salaries they receive. You can't take profit from a gravy train and at the same time try to destroy it."

Well actually that's pretty much what UKIP is doing, at least as far as our own membership is concerned. We make no apology for reclaiming just a tiny, tiny fraction of the vast sums of cash that Britain has shovelled into the EU's coffers, and using it to expose the rottenness within.

And if Bideford Labour Party (all three of them) took a short walk down-river they might realise that Appledore shipyard is now on a life-support machine thanks to EU rules preventing the UK government from favouring British shipbuilders over European ones, when competitors from France, Germany and Poland are propped up with illegal subsidies.

Given that the entire Lib/Lab/Con has now become a single party (with socialist Polly Toynbee from the Guardian a possible Tory advisor) I would have thought that UKIP's long-term success was pretty much assured.

January 2007

THE MANOR INN, AND OTHER VANDALISM

Back in 1967 there was a pub in Exeter's North Street, a real gold mine. One weekend, Sid, the owner, took nearly £1,500 across the bar. Serious money for those days. But when Sid retired, the new owner ignored his own core customers and took just 18 months to wreck the business.

It still happens. In the Devon village of Lower Ashton, in the Teign Valley, there was a wonderful old pub, with flagged floors, real ale, no music. The very walls breathed history. But new people recently moved in and gutted the place, obliterating the character, turning it into a Notting Hill wine bar. As one local commented: "Unbelievable". After this stupid act of vandalism, most people now shun the place, visiting other pubs in the valley.

It's the same at Widdecombe-in-the-Moor, where the Old Inn used to be a place of roaring fires, steaming dogs and a pleasing jumble of walkers and families tucking into trencherman-sized lunches. Alas, no more. The pub has been poncified, given the London treatment. Muddy boots unwelcome. Three café latte's please, and a soda water for Dominic.

The reason I'm droning on about vandalised watering holes is because they all ignored their core customer base and then paid the price. Tory leader David Cameron is making exactly the same mistake, converting the Conservative 'local' into a Notting Hill wine bar, complete with lava lamps and conceptual art; something that is shallow and transient.

Mr Cameron forgets, or does not care, that voters and party members can always drink elsewhere.

January 2007

HOOTS MON

At the next general election the British people will be faced by the three main political parties, and each one will be led by a Scot. The chances of this happening by accident are 1,728-to-1 against. Or a probability of 99.94% that it is deliberate policy. All very odd.

The Tory Party (with 134,446 members, or 0.22% of the population) plumped for David Cameron as new leader, ensuring that the English people must choose between three Scots, when only 1-in-12 citizens of the UK are Scottish.

When the Lib Dems (29, 697 members, another private club) ousted Mr Kennedy (another Scot) for Ming Campbell, they did it by an even smaller margin, just 0.05% of the population. And if Brown is crowned by Blair (as seems likely) we will have been presented with a choice of five Scots as leader, in succession. The chances of this happening by chance are 248,832-to-1. But if you include the Speakers of the House (that's right: they're both Scots) the odds become 35,831,808-to-1, and the probability of this being a deliberate plan rises to 99.996%... This amounts to racial discrimination, and I therefore demand an expensive, futile and time-consuming Public Inquiry to unearth the truth. Or perhaps not.

I have no problem with Scotland or Wales playing an active part in the culture of British politics, but it is crystal clear that Englishman are now being prevented from leading political parties in Britain.

But hold on a moment. There is one exception. Nigel Farage is leader of the UK Independence Party, and he's English through and through, so I clearly do not know what I'm talking about. Problem solved.

January 2007

(with thanks to Tom Knott Pallister).

MY BEST OF BRITISH

I received this letter at UKIP Head Office in November 2006, and thought you might like to read it, exactly as written...

"Dear Sir,

I was called up in 1941 at the age of eighteen, to assist in the prevention of my country being invaded. My so-called successive governments, especially in the last ten years, have ruined what was my country. What I

*now consider is my enemy – parliament – has forced
me to repay a portion of my meagre worked for pension
to pay for food, clothing, and keep for foreign invaders.*

*I have lost my freedom of speech. I have lost my
Human Rights. Most of my "Best of British" have died.
Many of my present "Best of British" have been forced
to emigrate.*

*I suppose that I will be released during the next ten
years, but I fear for the lives of our great grand
children.*

Do something about it, please".

January 2007

THE NEXT TURNING ON THE LEFT

The EU's satellite navigation system is called Galileo,
similar to America's Global Positioning System (or
GPS). Unlike Galileo, GPS is free to all customers
(though the enhanced military version is still Top
Secret) but the EU's version was meant to be a
money-spinner, with Brussels charging us for access
to the codes.

With true EU incompetence they have now blown it.
"Tecchies" at Cornell's GPS Laboratory recently
cracked and published the secret codes in just two
months. The EU went ballistic, claiming "infringement
of intellectual property". But to no avail.

Professor Mark Psiaki of the Cornell team explained:
"Imagine someone builds a lighthouse and I've gone by
and see how often the light flashes and measured
where the coordinates are. Can the owner charge me a
licensing fee for looking at the light? No. How is
looking at the Galileo satellite any different?"

This means that consumers will have free access for Galileo sat-nav devices, including hand-helds and those installed in vehicles. It also means that the EU's plans to reap a huge bonanza have been stuffed, mounted, and displayed on the mantelpiece.

There is a much darker side to this. Given the ease of cracking the Galileo codes, the more enhanced military codes will also have been deciphered by the Chinese (who are sleeping partners in the Galileo team, but were never intended to be given access to the military system)...

This begs a question. Will Brussels agree to shut down the entire Galileo system if any hostile power looks like using it against America? Remember that Washington has already threatened to shoot down Galileo satellites if necessary.

Doesn't this rather undermine the claim that the EU will guarantee peace in Europe?

February 2007

IN DEATH AS IN LIFE

Christian graves traditionally face eastwards, in the belief that the Second Coming of Jesus will be from that direction. But headstones at the new £2.5-million High Wood Cemetery in Bulwell, Nottinghamshire, will be plotted to face northeast, in line with Islamic faith. Moslems believe that the dead look over their shoulder to the holy city of Mecca, in Saudi Arabia towards the southeast.

Nottingham Christians who want to be buried facing east (in the direction of Jerusalem) will now have to pay the Council for "extra maintenance". The C. of E. (at last standing up for its beliefs) has finally spoken out: the Rev David Gray, from St John's Church, Bulwell, said: "All faiths should have their beliefs respected... It is an evolving cemetery and should be made for people of all faiths and certainly people of Christian faiths."

Rachel Farmer, spokeswoman for the Diocese of Southwell and Nottingham, added: "Positioning all the graves in the direction of Mecca conflicts with the long-standing Christian burial tradition of graves facing towards the east. We believe the people of Nottingham should have the opportunity to follow the Christian burial traditions if they choose to and the Christian faith should not be discriminated against in this way. The 2001 census showed that 70% of the population considered themselves Christian."

Nottingham Council was unrepentant: "In the first phase of development it has been agreed that the graves will face north-east. For people of Muslim faith this fits in with a religious requirement, but it will also ensure a tidy appearance for the site as a whole."

It seems that even in death, the British majority must give way to the demands of a vociferous and belligerent minority. C'est la vie, I suppose.

February 2007

HIP, HIP, HOORAY

Unemployed? Looking for a job? I have the very thing. Train as a Home Surveyor, as advertised in the Daily Mirror last December. I'll quote from the advert:

"Applicants urgently needed **now** to carry out the **compulsory** Energy Ratings assessments **legally required** for almost every house or flat being sold from next June. Up to 2-million properties every year will need to be visited by thousands of newly trained Home Inspectors who will carry out the Government's legally required **Home Information Pack**.... Average fee earning expectations are £130 for an Energy Rating and £200 for a Home Condition Report with up to 12 ratings or 8 Reports anticipated in a week. **No surveying experience is necessary**"

Let's pause, and then rewind the tape a moment. As if life isn't expensive enough, without an already vast increase in bureaucracy (most of it fuelled by EU rules and regulations) we are now going to be hit by Labour's crazy Energy Ratings Assessments, enforced by thousands of clueless jobs-worths. And if you're moving house, you will still need to pay for a survey, done by a surveyor, who knows how to survey, and has passed a professional surveying exam.

It's very simple. A UKIP government will scrap HIPs. We can find better ways to spend public money: on schools, hospitals, more prisons, decent pensions, proper boots for soldiers; you name it.

February 2007

SAUCE FOR THE GOOSE

The UK Independence Party has just been ordered to surrender £363,697 to the Electoral Commission because the gentleman who originally gave them the money – Alan Bown - had dropped off the electoral roll at the time he wrote the cheque. Mr Bown lives in Kent, not the Bahamas. He is a British businessman, employing British workers, and pays taxes and business rates in Britain. He is not a tax-exile nor a foreign donor (the reason these rules were brought in). Every donation to UKIP was properly recorded and reported.

The decision to take this money for what was merely a clerical error is deeply disturbing, verging on Stalinist. It does nothing for British democracy and is rightly seen by the public as a politically inspired attack on this small but growing Party. It also reflects badly on the Electoral Commission, bringing them into disrepute in the public eye. This was a classic "stitch up", as one member of the public – not a UKIP member - told me on the telephone the other day; and every caller echoed this. They were furious. People are not stupid; they recognise skulduggery when they see it.

I believe the Commission to be guilty of double standards. Perhaps they should take a closer look at our Prime Minister, who makes a habit of taking tea and questions at 10 Downing Street with the Metropolitan Police every Thursday afternoon?

Or consider the case of Michael Brown who recently gave £2.4 million to the Liberal Democrats; this came from his firm "5th Avenue Partners". But under election law company donations can only be accepted from companies "carrying on business in Britain". Individual donors must also be registered to vote in Britain. Michael Brown was not. He has since been jailed for two years for committing perjury and for making a false passport application...

This is rather more sinister than an innocent clerical error made by UKIP's Alan Bown. Yet amazingly the Lib Dems have been allowed to keep the £2.4 million. If you are getting a distinct smell of fish, then you are not alone.

March 2007

In a court judgement that Autumn , UKIP was ordered to repay £18,000

IN WHICH IS CONTAINED
A VERY LONG SENTENCE

I don't think I'm divulging State Secrets when I tell you that UKIP historically gets its support 25% from Labour voters, 25% from Tory, and the remaining 50% from Lib-Dems and those who don't normally take an interest in politics. But things have recently changed, and UKIP has welcomed an influx of disillusioned Tories who have suddenly realised that there is no difference between Cameron and Blair. And not all of them have been peers of the realm or high-profile advisors to Ken Clark.

Don't take it from me. Here is a recent letter to the Independent: "Sir, I despair of the Conservatives. They spurned at least three chances to appoint sensible David Davis as their leader, and have lumbered themselves with this namby-pamby, touchy-feely, pseudo-evangelical Tony Blair Mk2; just when we're sick to death of Blair.... It's the UKIP for me. *Brian Rushton*".

Hardly surprising really. David Cameron has utterly failed to demolish Labour for its neglect of our Armed Forces, wrecking of a prosperous economy, high taxes, destruction of personal pensions, rising interest rates, chaos in the NHS, failure of schools to teach children even how to read, and collapse of our borders through uncontrolled immigration and insane multiculturalism, not to mention the general breakdown of law and order; all of it to the accompaniment of a descending ground bass of subservience to Brussels which makes 80% of our laws and costs us a fortune in membership.

If you're looking for an antidote for New Labour you won't find it in David Cameron, I'm afraid. He's far too busy hugging hoodies or glaciers. No, Nigel Farage, leader of UKIP...he'd be your man.

March 2007

WHERE DUCKS PUT THEIR BILLS

If you thought that most politicians were further down the evolutionary scale than wheel-clampers, you'd be right. Despite the fact that Westminster MPs have recently voted themselves a 66% pay-rise, they are now trying to get you, the public, to fund their activities. This is called "State Funding For Political Parties", and you (and I) will be picking up the tab.

UKIP's position is quite simple: if British political parties lack the volunteers to support them, then they have no right to exist. They should be out there winning back their ex-members and gaining more, not expecting the taxpayer to bail them out. Parties in France and Germany have huge public funding, along with probably the worst political corruption scandals than in almost every other democracy on the planet. Francois Mitterrand and Helmut Kohl were both disgraced after their time in office.

You might be interested to know why this is happening. The three biggest parties (but particularly Labour and Tory) have raised money either by dodgy loans or cash for peerages. We have even seen Tony Blair interviewed by Scotland Yard in its fraud enquiry.

The Westminster Parties are now running scared, needing money like a desperate gambler who has just sold his family estate and is now considering blipping Great Aunt Agatha on the head for her Crown Derby plate. But in this case, dear reader, YOU are Aunt Agatha.

The figures from the independent Electoral Commission make it very clear. In a news release from November 2006, they revealed the annual loans, mortgages and credit facilities of British political parties: Conservative Party (£35,315,060)...Labour Party (£23,390,992).... Lib Dem (£1,131,277). In sharp contrast was UKIP, the fourth biggest party, with a mere £19,200.

The Conservatives have now paid off the debt by selling their London HQ in Smith Square (the last of the family silver has now gone) but the Labour Party will probably never, ever, be able to repay such a vast sum, so they will need **You** to pay off their mortgage.

March 2007

OFFICIAL GUIDANCE FOR FARMERS....

"Milk but no sugar, please. I'm behind a desk too much. We're very busy at the Ministry but it's good to get out and visit the 'sharp end'...You get a wonderful view of the farm from here, don't you? And that Aga chucks out some heat.

Now then, you need a *business plan*. Identify where you're strong. Times are hard for agriculture. The Ministry is aware of that. And you can't survive by farming. Mmm, these scones! Homemade? Wonderful.

The tractor must go, and most of the sheep and bullocks. Keep a few for the tourists; local colour and all that - bed & breakfast. But as a business they're passé, I'm afraid. Pity.

You look surprised, but that's why I'm here: advice from the horse's mouth, as it were. Survival's the game. Constant change is here to stay. It's all 'beef from Brazil and chickens from Thailand', until Bird

Flu at least. But you take the point... Oh yes, more tea, thank you, and another scone. Your own jam? Delicious!

Those barns across the yard. An asset. As low-cost housing, the local Planning Officer would certainly be on-side. Help the shortage. Everybody's fleeing the cities. You'll do well.

You're not convinced? Well, I suppose you are a little isolated here. Had you considered a theme park? How they USED to farm. Have a few locals from the village mooching around in smocks, sharpening billhooks, trying to be polite to the holidaymakers. But no, you're probably right. Bit cheesey really.

There are EU grants available for cactus farms, for when they decide global warming has properly got on-stream. You could begin down there, in the water meadow. A small plot. See how it goes. Very efficient, tax-wise. I'll look into it.

You could always sell the farmhouse. It's a London buyers dream. I see I've not convinced you, but what *marvellous* clotted cream."

April 2007

(With thanks to Hilary John)

WORDS TO THE WISE

This is an edited version of a speech given recently to an audience of high-school children, by the head of Microsoft, Bill Gates. He comes across as a born UKIP-supporter.

"Rule 1...Life is not fair. Get used to it.

Rule 2...The world won't care about your self-esteem.

The world will expect you to accomplish something BEFORE you feel good about yourself.

Rule 3...If you think your teacher is tough, wait till you get a boss.

Rule 4...Flipping burgers is not beneath your dignity. Your grandparents had a different word for it. They called it opportunity.

Rule 5...Before you were born your parents weren't as boring as they are now. They got that way from paying your bills, cleaning your clothes, and listening to you talk about how cool you are. Before you save the rain forest, try delousing your bedroom.

Rule 6...Your school may have done away with winners and losers but this doesn't bear the slightest resemblance to real life.

Rule 7... Television is not real life. In real life people actually have to leave the coffee shop and go to jobs.

Rule 8... Be nice to nerds. Chances are you'll end up working for one.

If you can read this, thank a teacher. If you are reading it in English, thank a soldier"...

Which pretty much says it all really.

April 2007

THE SQUIRREL AND THE GRASSHOPPER

The Real Life Version

A squirrel works hard through the long hot summer, building his house and storing away nuts for the winter. The grasshopper thinks he's a fool, and plays and dances the summer months away. In winter the squirrel is warm and well fed. The grasshopper has no food or shelter, and dies in the snow.

The PC British Version

A social worker finds the shivering grasshopper, and calls a press conference, condemning the squirrel for being warm while the grasshopper is cold and starving. The BBC provides live coverage of the desperate grasshopper with video cuts of the squirrel in his comfortable home. The public are brainwashed into feeling ashamed that the poor grasshopper could be allowed to suffer in such a wealthy country.

Unwilling to miss a passing bandwagon, the "Once Upon a Time Conservative Party" along with the "Grasshoppers' Green Alliance Forum" together stage a mass demonstration outside the squirrel's house. This results in the squirrel's taxes being "re-assessed" and the confiscation of his food stocks, which are then distributed to the needy (the grasshopper).

The squirrel, bowing to the inevitable, now moves to Spain to run a little taverna. Back in England his old house is seized by the local authority as a refuge for a group of asylum-seeking cats.

The felines had originally arrived in the UK after highjacking a plane from Katmandu. They were arrested, but then tried to blow up the airport after realising that eight out of ten British pet-owners (who expressed a preference) would rather keep dogs than cats. But the cats were released into the community when the BBC revealed to a stunned nation that the police had fed them pilchards instead of salmon.

This resulted in the new Liberal Democrat Government praising the cats for enriching Britain's multicultural diversity, and criticising the dogs for failing to befriend the cats.

Meanwhile in Spain, the squirrel flicks through the Sunday papers; and with a little clink of ice, lifts his 'Sundowner' in a toast to those he has left behind.

April 2007

With apologies to whoever wrote the (much longer) original version of this.

A FIRST CLASS STAMP

Before Brussels came along, the Post Office was that rare and unique thing: a State-owned monopoly that actually made a profit for the Treasury. It even included elements of a social service, maintaining some rural post offices and deliveries where (in all honesty) they weren't profitable. But overall it was a benefit to the community and the system worked. A letter delivered in London, subsidised one delivered to the Orkneys.

But then along came EU Directive 97/67/EC, which effectively split our Post Office into Parcelforce, Counters, and Royal Mail Letters. Firms like DHL and TNT moved in and cherry-picked the profitable city routes or those on good travel networks, leaving the poor old Post Office with the scrag-end...

How can Royal Mail possibly deliver a letter from Redruth to Stornaway for 24p and still make a profit? It can't, of course. And if you are left with the unprofitable part, you must dump the most expensive bits or go totally bust. That is why hundreds of rural and urban post offices have now drawn down the shutters, abandoning thousands of customers - many of them elderly or infirm. True, the rise of e-mail, fax, and texting on mobile phones means that fewer letters are being posted, but that makes an even stronger case for subsidising a nationwide service. Remember, the Police or Fire Brigade are not expected to turn a profit.

The newest round of closures (officially 2,500, though probably nearer 3,000) came from EU directive 2002/39/EC, a 20-page document which landed with a dull thump into the lap of Jack Straw, then Foreign Secretary. The document was "C(2003)1652 fin State Aid N784/2002".

This decision to axe another 3,000 outlets was made in Brussels, not London. And Neelie Kroes (EU Sub-Post Offices Competition Commissioner) then announced that she was "happy" to endorse a new agreement with the British Government to run until March 2008, which was very nice of her.

May 2007

MIRROR IN THE BATHROOM

At a private girl's school in Washington DC, the janitor faced a tricky problem. The girls, some as young as 12, were putting on lipstick and then pressing their lips to the mirror, leaving dozens of tiny lip-prints. Every night the Janitor scrubbed them off. Every morning they would reappear.

The Principal took action. She summoned the girls and the Janitor to a meeting in the washroom, and explained that the lip-prints were difficult to remove and posed a real problem for the cleaning staff.... To show the girls how much effort it took to clean the mirrors every night she asked the Janitor to give a demonstration.

He took out a long-handled squeegee, dipped it into the toilet, and cleaned the mirror with it. There have been no more lip-prints on the mirrors since then. As someone once said: There are teachers. And then there are educators.

May 2007

HOLDING UP A MIRROR

The Trago Column isn't usually a critical review, but please make an exception for an exceptional book...

If you buy only one serious title this year, may I recommend: "Holding Up a Mirror" by Anne Glyn-Jones, sub-titled How Civilisations Decline. This book will alter your whole view of history, yet manage to explain things in such a simple straightforward way you'll kick yourself for not spotting it sooner. And the more one reads, the clearer things become.

As one fan told her: "After reading your book, I was really cheered up. I've often wondered why things were going so wrong. Now I can see how it all hangs together. Even if I can't stop these things, at least now I understand WHY they are happening."

Anne Glyn-Jones takes the four great civilisations of Greece, Rome, Christendom, and the modern West;

and charts how each rose and fell. (Here in the UK we are probably living out the end phase of the British Empire; and the state of modern British TV supports her view)

She approaches it by studying the entertainment industry of each of these periods, particularly stage-plays and dramas of the time, though the spotlight also focuses on the mass spectacles of the Coliseum and the Hollywood film industry.

Glyn-Jones identifies a logical development in human societies, and explains why each blossoms, loses belief in itself, and then implodes. These civilisations eventually fall to attacks from outside; but the real demolition job was done earlier, by those within the walls.

Although it is not a "beach book", Holding Up a Mirror would certainly come with me to that mythical desert island, and be a good companion. This is a book to read, savour, and re-read through those long dark nights; though you'd need a good stock of candles.

'Holding Up a Mirror' is published by Imprint Academic.

(ISBN 0 907845 60 6)

May 2007

FAMILY VALUES

Sometimes it's very important to get things on record.

A friend of mine came across the words "Phone Bill" written in red ink in his diary. In his own words: "I knew seven or eight Bills but I couldn't tell which one it was. In the end I thought stuff it and forgot all about it. Three weeks later BT told me they'd cut me off if I didn't pay up. That's when I decided to write everything down properly from now on."

But there are exceptions to this. One local authority recently erected a sign above a communal swimming pool. The sign read: "This has been designated the shallow end". There was no corresponding notice at the deep end. Perhaps they thought you would find that out for yourself?

Or take John Hipkin, former Lib Dem mayor of Cambridge. Responding to Government plans to build 47,000 new homes in his area, he pointed out that the city needed more 3-and-4 bedroomed houses for families. This was a bad mistake in today's lunatic asylum of political correctness. The Lesbian, Gay, and Transsexual Group on the Council then demanded an official apology from Mr Hipkin for committing "Hetero-sexism - discrimination towards non-heterosexuals due to cultural bias". In true waffle-speak the leader of Cambridge Council, Mr Nimmo-Smith, said: "His remarks were capable of being interpreted as non-inclusive."

Read the above, and weep for a civilisation dying not with a bang but a whimper.

June 2007

TOTAL RUBBISH!

How very ironic. I see that Ben Bradshaw MP now wants us to have our refuse collected every fortnight. As Council Tax spiralled out of control, the rest of us could at least console ourselves with the thought: "Oh well, at least they take away the rubbish". Now they won't even take the bins on time.

It proves that New Labour is still the 'tax and spend' party. "If it moves (particularly in four-wheel-drive) then tax it. If it doesn't move, tax it anyway. The idiots'll pay."

The real difference is that at least Old Labour actually cared when they inevitably messed everything up because they couldn't run a bath. Mr Bradshaw's lot merely smile and carry on.

The UK Independence Party is totally committed to weekly rubbish collections. It is one of the basic core services expected from a council, and no amount of weasel words from Ben Bradshaw and his chums will alter that. The British people are paying through the nose for a bad service that is getting worse, and the sooner this utterly useless government is swept away the better for everyone... with the possible exception of Ben Bradshaw MP, who would lose his job.

But at least he'd get his bins emptied once a week, so he shouldn't be too downcast.

May 2007

MORE RUBBISH!

As Council Tax spiralled upwards, partly thanks to EU regulations, partly to the fact that we are governed by people who despise us, we could at least console ourselves with the thought: "Oh well, at least they take away the rubbish". But no longer. In order to avoid massive fines from Brussels (regarding landfill waste) we must recycle more and go over to fortnightly bin collections, despite huge public opposition.

We all hate needless waste – but this is not the way. Refuse collection is a core duty of the local council. We pay them to work for us, not the other way around.

If the Government is serious about recycling/pollution it must do two things. First, announce to all businesses that in, say, four years time every piece of packaging sold in Britain must be biodegradable. (We can't do that, because it's against the EU rules of the Single Market). Secondly, it must ensure that packaging is itself kept to the absolute minimum, perhaps through tax-breaks to the industry.

You might be interested in a few figures from around the world: UK's recycling rate 27%. In the USA, 32% (rubbish collections 2-3 times a week). In Switzerland 51% (collections 1-2 times a week), and in Spain 35% (daily collections in cities, three times a week elsewhere). Greece is also interesting. (20% recycling - the lowest rate in Europe – with daily collections in cities, but no compulsory recycling)... which shows that without recycling schemes it doesn't matter how often the bins are emptied. The two go together.

I will leave you with another little fact. To avoid paying huge fines to Brussels, the UK currently exports millions of tons of landfill waste to China, where the Chinese dump it into a big hole in the ground and shovel earth over the top, which is a perfect metaphor for our involvement with the EU.

June 2007

PIGS IN **SPACE!!!!!!!**

Billy Bragg (left-wing singer and political campaigner) makes a strange bed-fellow for the Bishop of Southwark (accused of drunken behaviour at a London party, you may recall) Baroness Shirley Williams, and Cardinal Murphy-O'Connor, head of the Roman Catholic Church in England. But surprisingly they came together on 7th May 2007 in Trafalgar Square to launch the "Strangers into Citizens" campaign.

The campaign proposes that all migrants who have been in Britain for more than four years should be given a 2-year work permit, then given indefinite leave to remain, if they sit an English test and can produce references. They were not alone. Thousands of supporters assembled, armed with placards reading: "ABOLISH ALL RACIST IMMIGRATION CONTROLS" and "NO-ONE IS ILLEGAL".

As useful as lipstick on a pig, this is an amnesty parading as a solution. And it will fail. Italy and Spain have each granted five amnesties in the last 20 years. All of them resulted in a further wave of immigrants. Here in Britain we have possibly one million illegal immigrants, let alone hundreds of thousands legally from EU states such as Poland, Rumania etc. Only UKIP voted to prevent this.

Even now, across the Channel the French are busily erecting Camp Sangatte Mk2. We have had enough warnings. The effects upon the NHS, social housing, low wages, sexploitation, working class anger, and urban crime are huge and increasing. The last thing we need is to advertise to the world: "Come on in – Billy Bragg said it's OK."

June 2007

I AM TAKING YOUR BULLDOZER INTO CUSTODY

If you want to see the real nature of the EU, then here we go. On 24th June four UKIP MEPs were threatened with arrest by uniformed goons as they protested outside the European Union summit.

The MEPs were Nigel Farage (UKIP leader), John Whittaker, Derek Clark, and Gerard Batten. They had brought along a giant rubber inflatable bulldozer. On the shovel-blade were the words: "Clearing the way for the new Constitutional Treaty".

Cue the Belgian police, led by Divisional Commander Pierre Vandernissen, who told the MEPs he was taking the bulldozer into custody. He explained he was: "acting on higher instructions". The MEPs asked why? Answer: "Because I have the power." which was less than illuminating.

Jeremy Paxman would have relished it: "Oh come on, Inspector. Surely you don't expect us to swallow *that* as an explanation!"

By this time 35 cops had pitched up just yards from the entrance to the European Council's marvellously named "Zone of Free Expression". A wagon train of police vans then formed a ring around the rubber bulldozer, obscuring the view of the world's TV cameras.

When Mr Farage objected he was informed: "You will go to a cell for 12 hours and then we will sort it out". The same cop later threatened to arrest everyone in the area, including the press. All because he "had the power", one must assume. But then that is the real face of 'Europe'.

I'll leave the last word to Nigel Farage: "Once again we have seen that the EU don't want to know about concerns people may have. They can't accept that NO means NO, which is why they are holding discussions over this treaty in secret, and are trying to sneak in parts of the EU Constitution even though the French and Dutch voted against it. How Labour, Conservatives and Liberal Democrats can want to hand over more power to these people is, frankly, astonishing."

July 2007

LOW FAT YOGHURT AND A GLASTONBURY PORTALOO

Over the last few years the Trago column has been "banging on" about the destruction of British farming. And no apologies for that. Hitler's U-boats nearly won, because they cut off most of our food supplies. Food security is vital. But our urban-based Labour government still thinks that bacon comes from Sainsburys.

Take the dairy industry (why not? everyone else has). We once had the Milk Marketing Board. A monopoly that worked, just like the Post Office; and both were crippled by the EU. The Post Office still has another three years or so before it finally dies. But the Milk Marketing Board is already dead and gone, a dusty memory, along with most dairy farming.

A case in point. Her Majesty the Queen is patron of the Ayrshire Cattle Society. But now even she is admitting defeat and selling up. The Windsor Ayrshire herd has grazed Home Park on the Windsor Estate for 56 years, but now it's up for grabs. A Royal spokesman said:

"There have been significant losses over several years, with milk prices failing to cover the high cost of production". The price was 19p a litre, but production costs were at least 22p.

The Competition Commissioner is investigating the low prices paid to farmers by supermarkets and processing companies, but many farmers are reluctant to give evidence to the inquiry, fearing that they will lose contracts. It makes you wonder though: with such suicidally low prices the long-term prospects are about as appealing as a Glastonbury portaloo. If I was a dairy farmer I'd be greatly tempted to give most of the supermarkets a spring-loaded V-sign from the hip... and go into yoghurt.

July 2007

THE CRACK IN THE DAM

I've just been to a meeting at County Hall in Exeter.... It was spellbinding. You should have come. We were watching the unelected SW Regional Assembly: faceless, grey paper-pushers, arrogant yet complacent. The UK Independence Party has fought them for years. But at this meeting, something was different. The delegates were shocked. Stunned. "Why?" I hear you ask. I'll tell you. One day earlier Gordon Brown had poured a pot of cold tea all over their bonfire, announcing that expensive quangoes like the SW Regional Assembly would be abolished. And now the delegates were panicking. Headless chicken time.

Like ferrets in a sack, they turned on each other. "Where is the Minister for the South West?" they demanded. "Why isn't he here?" But of newly promoted Ben Bradshaw there was no sign. Bigger fish to fry.

Another delegate briefly cheered them up: "The Government cannot just shut down this Assembly." At this point in London, Gordon Brown pressed a button and the Exeter delegate's chair dropped him into a tank of barracuda in the cellar. There was brief splashing, then into the silence a dour voice intoned: "I'm Prime Minister laddie. Wi a mandate. Which is more than this chamber o'hot air has ever had! The lot of ye are history!"

A third perspiring delegate, running a finger around his loosened collar, mentioned finance: "We in the Communities Parish Organisation demand that our original financial investment appears separately in the accounts of the SWRA". Translated this means: "How much of our cash is trapped inside this crock of wotsit, and how do we get it out before the fat lady sings?"

Graham Booth UKIP MEP used his allotted 3 minutes on the platform to wish the SWRA a happy retirement, eliciting good-natured laughter and a round of applause from the public gallery. He also reminded each member of the SW Regional Assembly that in all probability they will be incurring personal liability for the £-1 million debt that would otherwise be paid by taxpayers. Ashes to ashes, dust to dust. Requiest in pace, oh SWRA, but you will not be missed.

July 2007

WAS OLD ENOCH RIGHT?

Thomas Llewellyn Jones owns a fish and chippie named 'Llew's Takeaway', in Bridgend, Wales. Mistaking him for a Chinese, Ashuk Miah an 'advocate' of the Newport Immigration Advice Centre, sent him a business letter in April 2007. Before I quote the exact words of this advert, please *move heavy objects out of reach, lest you feel a sudden urge to throw them out the window*.

The letter introduces NIAC as: "an independent immigration advisory service for: Advice and application on how to bring your elderly parents or relatives to visit United Kingdom... Advice on how to bring people on work permit... On how to bring newly married wife or husband to UK... On how to bring students to UK... On how to bring elderly people to UK for medical treatment... Application to stay in UK indefinitely if you entered as a newly married spouse.... Application to extend present stay in UK if a visitor.... Application for naturalisation as a British Citizen.".

Miah concludes with the comforting news: "If any of the above applications are refused, I can lodge an appeal on your behalf".

And the depressing truth is that Miah is right. Our Government has surrendered control of our borders (partly thanks to the EU, partly to the insane Human Rights Act, also EU-inspired); hence businesses like the Newport Immigration Advice Centre. I never thought that I would quote Enoch Powell in the Trago column, but here we go: On Britain's immigration policy (and this was 30 years ago): "It is like watching a nation heaping up its own funeral pyre."

I now have a distinct feeling that despite all the bad press, Powell might just have been right all along.

July 2007

THE SPIRIT OF RADIO

On Radio Devon's 'Justin Leigh' show (26th June) the presenter read out an email from a lady listener: "Every week we are subjected to a barrage of anti-EU rants from Trago in the newspapers, but most of the staff seem to be Polish".

One person's 'rant' is another's reasoned argument I suppose, but I must defend Bruce Robertson employing workers from Eastern Europe.

Only UKIP voted "NO" to the enlargement of the EU. The others all voted "YES". But there's a huge difference between granting temporary work permits for passing labour, and the EU (actually Blair's) decision of granting them full citizenship rights, with all the knock-on effects.

For Trago, it's also a business matter. They face the problem of a British labour-force which, to be brutally honest, doesn't want to work in a shop. And the benefits system here in Britain makes it easy for the work-shy to sit with their hands out, when - again to be brutally honest - they should get off their subsidised backsides and start working in the real world. The only place where money grows on trees is Brussels, where cash magically appears and is dispensed throughout "Europe" by an ineffably generous EU (just so long as you erect a sign saying "funded by the European Union").

Two of the biggest objections to hiring foreign labour are if the incomers take jobs from the indigenous people (but in this case, they don't). And secondly, if the money earned then leaves Britain and ends up in Poland. Continuing the 'brutally honest' theme, this probably happens. But give Bruce Robertson a break here. Would you rather they signed a contract that all salaries must be spent in Britain? That would be illegal anyway.

The UK Independence Party believes in the freedom of business to do the (legal) things necessary to survive, for the good of all. And if that means that foreign workers are temporarily required, then so be it. Let's use them. Like it or not, we live in a capitalist society, which means buying things cheaply and selling them slightly less cheaply.

And finally, to that rather angry lady who emailed Justin Leigh's phone-in programme, my sincere apologies if this comes across as a rant. All I'm doing is asking you to think

July 2007

RELOCATION, RELOCATION, RELOCATION

If you want to move abroad to Afghanistan, Pakistan, Nigeria, Iraq etc, here is the definitive guide how to do it...

Ignore immigration quotas, visas, international law etc. Once you arrive, demand free medical care for your family, and bilingual doctors, nurses, and teachers. Fly the Union Jack from your car. Demand classes in British culture in the Muslim school system. Speak only English at home, and insist that your children do the same.

Don't stop there. You'll need a driving licence, so show them your existing UK document and demand a local equivalent. If they object, then shout loudly enough and they will understand. Then drive around without car insurance and ignore local traffic rules. When the locals complain (and they will) organise protest marches against your host country, inciting violence against the institutions of the country that originally let you in (the government, police, TV companies, publishing houses, newspapers, Royal Family etc. Any of them will do).

But one word of warning. If you follow this advice, you'll probably end up dead. The above could only happen in the soft, politically correct West, where we are so terrified of offending anyone that we have totally lost any sense of reality.

August 2007

A DODGY HIP

The UK Government has now dropped its HIPs (or Home Information Packs: a sort of Green MOT for every house in Britain, designed to stop the icecaps melting on Mars). As usual, they planned badly, lacked the manpower, and have temporarily restricted HIPs to 4-bedroomed houses or larger. Again, the EU was behind it, another directive from Brussels costing us £-billions every year.

Typically our own government "gold-plated" it, making things far worse. Brussels originally wanted us to have new HIPs every ten years. But Tony Blair insisted that a new Energy Performance Certificate be commissioned every time the house is sold. Thank you, ex-Prime Minister Enjoy your retirement.

Here is a cut-down version of a recent letter to the Western Morning News by Mike John, from Winkleigh in Devon:

"My 16th Century, grade II listed farmhouse is of cob

construction with a thatched roof. The leaded windows are original and come complete with ventilation gaps, as do the doors. Heating is via a wood-burner and Aga. The house is naturally warm in the winter and cool in the summer, with a degree of dampness essential for its well-being. I defy anybody outside of a yurt to compete with what I have to buy and burn... I could conform to modern energy requirements and install double-glazing, draught excluders and central heating. An expert from Torridge Council would be able to advise how to put a damp course in a cob wall and solar panels in a thatched roof. But then two things would happen...

First, a different expert from TDC would take me to court for desecration of a listed building. Second, the house will fall down".

Mr John is spot on, but it's also a striking metaphor for our membership of the EU, which introduced this expensive lunacy in the first place.

August 2007

NEWS FROM THE ANTIPODES

This is yet another letter that I received at UKIP, and I thought you might be interested...

"I am currently in New Zealand on a visit to family and friends. However, would you believe it, it is another Socialist Utopia. Absolutely everything that has been inflicted on the UK is happening here – in particular uncontrolled idiotic immigration and a minority Socialist Govt. Only difference, the Finance Minister has also taxed heavily and built up a large nest egg in order to bribe the electorate at the next general election. HOME FROM HOME"....

As a postscript to that, I understand that five hundred British families a month have been emigrating to New Zealand to escape the violence, sleaze and crime of New Labour's fiefdom. But if this letter is true, then they might be jumping from the frying pan into the fire. I have a strong suspicion that we are obliged to stand and fight here in Britain. Running away only encourages them to follow, trying the same trick again.

September 2007

MIND YOUR P's AND Q's

Ten old friends met for a drink every weekend at the pub. They usually spent £100, so they worked out a system. The first four paid nothing. The fifth paid £1. The rest paid more according to their wealth. The tenth (the richest) paid £59...

One day the landlord came up to them: "I've been thinking. You're good customers – from now on I'm going to cut your bill by £20. Beer for the evening will now cost £80."

They kept the same rules for paying their share, so the first four still paid nothing. The rest divided the £20 windfall in a fair manner. They decided to reduce the remaining six shares by the same amount. For example, the seventh man now paid £5 instead of £7. The ninth paid £14 instead of £18. The tenth man (the richest) paid £49 instead of £59.

When they got outside, the seventh man started to complain: "I only got £2 out of that extra £20". And the eighth man joined in: "That's right. I only got three quid back when he", pointing to the richest man, "got

£10 – it's not fair. The rich get all the breaks!". The four poorest then chimed in: "The system exploits the poor. We didn't get anything at all."

The nine of them surrounded the tenth and beat him to a pulp. Next week he didn't turn up. So the rest of them sat down for an evening's beer. When the bill came they couldn't raise enough cash to pay even half.

To quote Professor David Kamerschen, Professor of Economics at the University of Georgia: "And that, boys and girls, journalists and college professors, is how the tax system works. The people who pay the highest taxes get the most benefit from a tax reduction. Tax them too much, attack them for being wealthy, and they may just not show up anymore. In fact they might start drinking overseas where the atmosphere is more friendly."

Please remember that there is no such thing as "Government Money" or "EU Funding". It all comes from the pocket of somebody who made it in the first place.

September 2007

THE LONG MARCH

John Prescott once said: "The Green belt is a Labour achievement, and we mean to build on it", but it's a cheap shot on my part. Prescott was only there as a fig leaf to Labour's Working Class voters, and his gaffes are so numerous that I (almost) feel guilty mentioning them. But while we're at it, my favourite is what he's meant to have said after a rough flight: "It's great to be back on terra cotta."

I'm sorry. I'll stop it. The reason for mentioning Prescott is that there is a vast difference between him and Gordon Brown, who is a clever, hard-working and generally bright man. Idiots don't become Prime Minister... True, he has destroyed our pensions industry, so that anyone with both cash and brains is now putting everything into property, but we'll pass on that for now.

The point is that Gordon Brown is refusing to hold a referendum on the renamed EU Treaty (read Constitution). At the time of writing forty Labour MPs and four large Trades Unions are in revolt, along with the Tories, UKIP, the Liberal Party, the CIB, and the cross-party Democracy Movement (not to mention the Sun, the Daily Mail, and the Daily Telegraph. Even the Guardian is starting to get in on the act).

For Gordon Brown to ignore this is a colossal mistake, beyond belief in its cack-handedness. Prescott, yes. Brown, I would never have believed it. Why break an election pledge?

On Saturday October 27th the Pro-Referendum Rally will be holding a march in London. They need every person in Britain who cares about this surrender of our sovereignty to come to the capital and protest. It doesn't matter whether you are Labour, Tory, UKIP, Lib Dem, even George Galloway's Respect Party. This is too important for petty political differences.

For details please visit
www.proreferendumrally.co.uk.

Think of it this way: at least it'll make a change from your usual Saturday!

September 2007

A CUDDLE FROM NEW LABOUR

Alistair Campbell was New Labour's master of spin. In his diaries he describes the way they approached things. He and Blair instinctively knew, instinctively recognised, that the Great Britain of 1997 had lapped up Big Brother and Pop Idol, celebrating celebrity for its own sake. Britain didn't want a leader. It wanted a cuddle. The message was: "Vote Labour – we're nicer than that horrible lot."

New Labour's media approach was more Richard & Judy, than Newsnight or Panorama. As biographer Stephen Pollard wrote recently: "Nothing illustrates how perfectly suited the fundamental shallowness of New Labour was to the modern electorate than the one occasion when Blair ignored its triviality, in the aftermath of 9/11. He was firm on Iraq....And he was repaid with a kick in the political groin by an electorate for which such things are far too troubling to be thinking about. [Alistair Campbell] has exposed, unwittingly, the deliberate emptiness at the heart of New Labour – and at the heart of a Britain which lapped it up."

Mr Pollard is a gifted writer, and I think he has a point (even if Iraq has become a near-total disaster). We get the politicians we deserve. It seems that back in 1997 much of Britain wanted to be governed by nannies, treated like imbeciles. The downside is that 300,000 Britons fled abroad last year, mostly to Spain, or Australia and other Commonwealth countries. This is a terrible waste of the very people – many of them entrepreneurs - needed to get us back on our feet once we leave the EU and start repairing the huge damage it has wrought upon our country.

September 2007

GIVE A DOG A BONE

In 1965 the American psychologist Martin Seligman made a discovery... He was repeating an established experiment, which involved sounding a bell, then giving a dog a mild electric shock. In time the dogs associated the bell with the shock and jumped up in anticipation of what was coming.

Seligman noticed something odd. After conducting the test a few times the dogs stopped jumping. They simply lay down and waited for the shock, even if the kennel door was left open. They had given up hope.

He realised that when a creature believes it has no control over its situation and whatever it does is futile, it stops fighting back. The same happened in the concentration camps when the inmates lay down to die, and can be seen today in floods and famines when the victims are so traumatised they are unable to fend for themselves. This is called Learned Helplessness.

I suggest that the government has now adopted this same technique against us, hoping that we'll lie down and give up: they claim to be listening, but ignore us, pursuing their own agenda. The re-named EU Treaty (read Constitution) is a case in point. Labour's 2005 election-winning manifesto promised a referendum on it. But Gordon Brown has betrayed that promise, is terrified of asking us, and clearly doesn't give a tinker's cuss what you think.

Seligman observed something else: Not all dogs gave up. About a third continued to resist the shocks. In human political terms many would be UKIP-supporters, with a make-up of resistance and independence. Are you one of them, or have you now rolled over, paws in the air?

September 2007

NOT WITH A BANG...

Some people can't help meddling. Take Lord Justice Sedley, one of our most left-wing judges. He wants the whole UK population to have its DNA recorded on the police national database. Justice Sedley is a former Communist – his old chambers, Cloisters, were known as 'the Kremlin'. In the 1970s he even tutored at the Communist University in London. It seems to me that he should stick to the day job, not try to introduce new laws suitable for George Orwell's vision of the future. Needless to say, UKIP is totally opposed to his proposals and will fight them while we draw breath.

The other recent example is Lord Malloch Brown recommending that Britain should surrender its seat on the UN Security Council. He stated in Brussels that he is a "huge fan of the European Union having just one place at the international table. I think it will go in stages, institution by institution. It is not going to happen with a bang". But he wants it to happen "as quickly as possible".

The problem here is that Malloch Brown is a top government adviser, yet his language deliberately undermines Britain's independence. In another age, this would be treason and he would have gone to the Tower, deservedly so in my view - he can be grateful for a more enlightened age. But this is not just a case of one man's personal opinion; this really matters because he is **employed to advise our Prime Minister**.

As William Hague said: "It is alarming that Gordon Brown has chosen to put in charge of UN reform the man who thinks we should give up our UN Security Council seat to the EU."

I agree with William Hague. Personally I'd rather give my plumber the job. At least he could handle any leaks.

October 2007

TIGER, TIGER

You could be forgiven for thinking that Labour and the Tories are the same. So who to vote for? The Greens, or BNP, UKIP, even the Lib Dems? Many people choose Lib Dem as a safe protest vote, but remember that they want "More Europe" than the others. So if you love Brussels, you must **VOTE LIB DEM**! Personally, I will avoid them like an overworked cliché.

As an example of their antics, we recently had MP Richard Younger-Ross (Lib Dem, Teignbridge) wanting to pull Britain out of the Eurovision Song Contest because the voting was skewed and unfair. Fine. But our membership of the European Union is far more damaging than if Chirpy Booma Bang gets the elbow from Eastern Europe. A sense of proportion might be useful here.

Just down the road from Mr Younger-Ross, may I present Torbay Councillor Colin Charlwood (another Lib Dim) who declared in 2006 that Torquay's palm trees were a health hazard; the palm leaves could scratch a passer-by's face or even poke out an eye.

Councillor Charlwood explained: "It's a bit like keeping tigers. They are beautiful to look at, but you wouldn't want them wandering the streets". To quote Richard Littlejohn (Littlejohn's Britain) "it borders on clinical insanity – You don't get a lot of tigers in Devon. Councillor Charlwood clearly belongs in a padded cell wearing a jacket".

October 2007

*In fairness to the Lib Dems - and you won't hear **that** very often - Mr Charlwood is now an Independent.*

THE FINAL BREAKING POINT

I am finally cured of Global Warming...

It came just before Christmas, listening to an interview with a climatologist on Radio 4's Today programme. I didn't catch the great man's name, but that's probably irrelevant. With great solemnity he announced that methane from the rear of farmyard cows was "a not inconsiderable factor in Global Warming". For me, this was the final breaking point (if you'll pardon the pun).

Yes, the Earth is warming up at the moment, with ice-caps melting and dormice waking in December, but the point about Climate Change is that climates change; it's in their nature. The Romans were growing oranges in Kent 2,000 years ago, and had vineyards as far north as Yorkshire. As for rising sea levels, Isle Brewers, Isle Abbots, and Athelney on the Somerset levels were, indeed, once islands; and Wareham was the Roman's main port on the South West coast. Today you are lucky to get to Wareham drawing 6ft of water on a big tide, and Roman ships drew far more than that.

In 1275 Danish explorers discovered Greenland and gave it that name because it was green and they could cultivate corn there. From 1500 to 1700 there was a mini ice-age, hence the paintings of skaters enjoying themselves on the frozen River Thames.

The icecaps on Mars are melting at the same rate as those on Earth, without the benefit of the internal combustion engine.

Even the North Sea was once a low-lying plain until "global warming" caused the oceans to flood in, hundreds of thousands of years before the invention of four-wheel-drive.

In the 1970s, scientists warned of a new Ice Age. When that didn't happen they switched to the ozone layer, which is now repairing itself. Today, academics who need cash for a research grant, must sign up to the dogma: "Global Warming is Caused by Man". Those who disagree are 'mavericks' or 'barking'. A bad sign.

Al Gore's film "An Inconvenient Truth" contained more holes than gruyere cheese but they still awarded him a Nobel prize. I wonder if the real motive was to put one in the eye of George Bush Junior, for winning the U.S. election by a hanging chad and then invading Iraq? Could that have had anything to do with it? Do you think?

I now believe that the whole thing is a self-perpetuating con, with the purpose of extracting taxes and exercising control over the populace. The moral blackmail is designed to make heretics feel guilty: "Don't you WANT to save the planet?"

Just for the record: I hate pollution, support recycling, and value clean seas and countryside; and if I ever take up farming, it will be organic (and I'm no tree-hugger). But the idea of Britain relying on wind turbines and bicycles just as China has become the third biggest market for Rolls Royce, is muddle-headed.

I suggest that "Global Warming Caused by Man" is all about taxing and controlling us, and needs to be challenged constantly. But even if you disagree, at least acknowledge the possibility. As for "backfiring cows" let's both consign that to the trashcan.

October 2007

NOT SMOKING CAN BE
BAD FOR YOUR SANITY

In April 2007 a party of fifteen British sailors were seized by Iranian guards in the Shatt-Al-Arab waterway. Our boys (and one girl, Fay Turney,) were treated abysmally. When they first got home the MOD permitted them to sell their stories to the highest bidder, but then changed its mind when the proverbial hit the revolving air-agitator.

We can argue whether the sailors should have stuck to "name, rank, and number". Their ordeal must have been unpleasant. One of the hostages even revealed that the Iranians "flicked" the back of his head, "nicked" his iPod, and "joked" that he looked like Mr Bean. But it's not like being captured by the Taliban, when your life expectancy can be measured in terms of how long it takes to sharpen up a scimitar.

More worrying than Britain's total humiliation to the whole world, was the reaction of Patricia Hewitt, then Health Secretary: "It is deplorable", she lamented, "that the woman hostage should be shown smoking. This sends completely the wrong message to our young people!"

Had I been one of those captured sailors, the first thing I'd have wanted is a jolly old gasper. Patricia Hewitt seems to have lost the plot. As THE WEEK magazine reported: "A line between civilisation and madness has been crossed here". Yet many of you will STILL vote Labour at the next election. Frankly it's beyond me. Totally barking.

October 2007

A PEANUT-PUSHING CUBICLE MONKEY

Are you fluent in New-speak?

Probably not, but let's see. 'Shooting the Puppy' is Corporate Management-Speak for saying the unsayable (rather like being opposed to the EU). Or how about to 'knife and fork it' (doing the job bit by bit)? But don't show option paralysis in the office (being unable to decide) or your boss might suspect you're a cubicle monkey, suffering from knowledge pollution, ready for assisted departure.

Far better to bow your head to TIIC (the idiots in charge) and eat your lunch al-desko (a cornflakes deskfast shows commitment) avoiding any CLM's (career limiting moves) along the way.

If you're a road warrior (or travelling salesman) stick to eating a' la car/dashboard dining but avoid being out of the loop for too long. And be sure to demonstrate your poly-attentiveness and ability for being an ideas hamster, capable of light-bulb moments which push the peanut forward.

These gems, and many more, can be found in Tony Thorne's entertaining book, Shooting the Puppy. As a committed opponent of the European Union, I'd like to be able to blame Brussels for this abuse of a perfectly good language. But not this time. This time it comes mostly from America, and we need to bear that in mind.

November 2007

WE DON'T LIVE ON AN ISLAND

In 1995 a BBC news journalist was interviewing a member of the Conservative Government: "Minister, could it be that Britain might actually prosper outside Europe?"

"Impossible", came the spluttering reply. "We don't live on an island."

Well actually we do live on an island. Walk far enough in any direction and even a senior Tory will get their feet wet. And living on that island has proved jolly handy for most of the time (apart from one little glitch in 1066 or thereabouts).

What I find most disturbing is that UKIP has been warning about the EU for the last decade, and the political parties and media have waved it away, dismissing it as xenophobia or racism. Now the sky is full of chickens coming home to roost, and Westminster politicians are suddenly waking up to the fact that membership of the EU means surrendering our rights to self-government. We cannot deport EU criminals. We cannot deport terrorists if their human rights might be offended. Most of our laws are now made in Brussels, and Gordon Brown is preparing to deliver us trussed up like a turkey, with the words: "It's only for a few days. The Constit... ah, the Treaty is nothing to worry about."

I am reminded of the words of Benjamin Disraeli, describing the Liberal Government of the day: "As I sat opposite the Treasury Bench, the Ministers reminded me of one of those marine landscapes not very unusual on the coasts of South America. You behold a range of exhausted volcanoes: not a flame flickers on a single pallid quest, but the situation is still dangerous. There are occasional earthquakes, and ever and anon the dark rumbling of the sea."

He could have been describing the Labour front bench of today.

November 2007

WHEN IN ROME

There's an old Italian proverb: "He who follows the limper, soon will limp". And it's come true in Britain today. In 1994 Learco Chindamo knifed his headmaster to death outside the school gates. The victim, Phillip Lawrence, bled to death on the pavement.

Cindamo went to prison for murder, but is now set to be freed and given a house, a new identity and ongoing police protection. And we'll be paying for it. We cannot deport him, sending him back to his native Italy, because it breaks EU law. Nothing to do with the Human Rights Act, as the politicians and the media tried to pretend.

Under the 2004 Citizens Directive, no matter how violent or terrible the crime, so long as a criminal has lived in this country for five years or more (even behind bars) Britain can never deport them if they are a European citizen. Like the Italian limper, this is self inflicted.

Tory leader David Cameron had an open goal, a total sitter, a gift. Visibly he girded his loins, strapped on his buckler and sallied forth into battle, condemning the Human Rights Act and the irresponsibility of the

Government. But then an aide whispered into his ear: "Psst, David...It's **_European_** law. Nothing we can do", and Cameron quietly hung up his sword and sat down again.

The same applies to Immigration and those viewing us as destination of choice. It's no good stopping immigrants coming in from the rest of the world, because all they'll do is arrive in Eastern Europe, get EU citizenship, and travel here quite legally.

You might be interested in the comments of Liam Byrne, UK Minister of State for Borders and Immigration: "I've got to be candid. Since we stopped counting people coming in and out of the country, it's much more difficult to be accurate."

November 2007

Mr Byrne made his comment on Channel 4 news 29/10/07

SEEING RED

When New Labour denies a story, that usually means the story is true and you can believe every word. It's a shame that 'spin' has led to this total breakdown of trust, but there you go. Pity really.

The Department of Culture, Media and Sport decided in late September that the Red Arrows display team would be banned from flying at the 2012 London Olympics. The reason? The jets were "unsuitable", "might offend other nations" and were "not in keeping with the event as they were too militaristically British."

The Red Arrow pilots were gob-smacked: "We have been simply blown away by this decision. For years we've talked about performing a display at the Olympic Games and how magnificent it would be. It never crossed our minds that we'd be banned."

After national outrage the Government went into a flat spin, out of control, transfixed by panic. "No decision has been made," spluttered a spokesman for the dept, followed by the sounds of furious back-pedalling and muffled demands behind closed doors for the Tippex stick.

Next we had accusations in the House, with the Government pointing the finger at the Opposition. "You leaked this story to the Press!" The Conservatives just grinned, enjoying the moment.

But even if the story had been pure invention...which it wasn't... how very telling on this lousy Government that it rang so horribly true that everyone immediately and instinctively believed it.

November 2007

WINDS OF CHANGE

In late 2006 the Government approved plans to build a gigantic wind farm in the Thames Estuary. There were to be 341 turbines, plus another 100 seven miles off Margate. Greenpeace praised the idea: "It is clean energy on a massive scale. It's a pioneering project and we need more of them.".... But may I suggest that although we want clean energy, sometimes it's not that simple.

UKIP's Jeffery Titford is an MEP for the area. He responded to Greenpeace with an article called Winds of Change: "I beg to differ. Have Greenpeace given a moment's thought to the impact on the marine environment of drilling 341 holes in the seabed and filling them with concrete and metal? What about the hundreds of miles of cable that will have to be laid on the seabed to link all these metal monstrosities to land. How about the energy that goes into manufacturing turbines, which takes years to achieve payback?"

Jeffrey has a point. He went on: "Local fishermen are up in arms as there will be significant disruption to fish shoals and spawning areas, with long-term changes to the water flow and disturbance of organisms that live on the bottom, in turn affecting food for fish and shellfish. Then there's the affect on migrating birds... I could go on."

Jeffrey finished with a final salvo: "The rush to build turbines is symptomatic of a Government obsession that defies common sense. Figures from the Renewable Energy Foundation show that land-based turbines operate on only 28% efficiency. The figures are more like 23% in Cornwall and Wales. I am as interested in preserving the environment as anybody, but I prefer a more realistic approach, rather than wholesale environmental vandalism in pursuit of a green myth."

It's certainly something to think about. Everything comes with a price. The question is, can we afford to buy?

December 2007

AHEM...

FOR MY EUROPHILE READERS...

Please accept with no obligation my best wishes for an environmentally sustainable, socially cohesive, non-judgemental and gender-neutral celebration of the ensuing Winter solstice, regardless of your own religious (or, indeed, non-religious) observances.

I wish you a fiscally rewarding, individually satisfying experience of the forthcoming Western calendar year 2008, although this implies no criticism of those who observe a different calendar.

Without regard to the race, creed, colour, age, physical disability or sexual orientation of anyone subject to this communication, this greeting implies no commitment to implement personally any of the aforesaid wishes, nor are they guaranteed for more than twelve months. The wisher reserves the right to withdraw said wishes without notice and asserts sole intellectual property rights over their content.

AND FOR EVERYONE ELSE......................

Merry Christmas and a very, very Happy New Year!!!!!!!!!!!!

December 2007

(With many thanks to Ian Bannister)

Acknowledgements

"I must acknowledge the efforts of a number of people who have mined deeply into the workings of the EU and provided much of the raw material for this book. Not all of them are fans of UKIP, but their dedication to the cause of "withdrawal from the EU" is undeniable and it would be wrong not to thank them... even if we may sometimes disagree on the best way of achieving it.
Hats off to Dr Richard North, Christina Speight, Daniel Hannan MEP, Iris Binstead, the late Pam Barden (a true, gutsy fighter who is much missed),Ian Bookless,and Nigel Farage MEP. There are many others, and many, many thanks to all of you.

David Challice   February 2008"